Introduction

This book supports students preparing for the OCR AS examination. Written by experienced practitioner and mathematician, this comprehensive set of practice papers offers thorough preparation for the OCR assessment. Each practice paper is in line with the OCR syllabus and exam board specifications, and provides a rich and varied practice to meet all requirements of the OCR AS level Mathematics.

Papers are designed to teach students applicable, reusable and faster solutions to common problems. Each paper utilises problems to target areas of mathematics which students often find more difficult in the exam. Solutions provided have been reviewed by many students to ensure that they are easily understandable while being the fastest and most re-applicable.

The practice papers cover the following eleven distinct topics:

1. Proof
2. Algebra and functions
3. Sequences and series
4. Exponentials and logarithms
5. Coordinate geometry
6. Trigonometry
7. Vectors
8. Calculus
9. Statistics, probability and statistical hypothesis testing
10. Kinematics
11. Forces and Newton's laws

After completing these practice papers, you should be able to:

1. Formulate optimal solutions quicker to any OCR AS level Mathematics question
2. More readily apply previously learnt skills on a question to question basis

The OCR AS level Mathematics practice papers comprises of 2 books, books 1 and 2, for Papers 1 and 2 in the OCR, respectively. Each book contains 4 full practice papers and solutions.

Contents

Instructions

- Time allowed for each paper: 1 hour and 30 minutes.
- Use black ink. HB pencil may be used for graphs and diagrams only.
- You are permitted to use a scientific or graphics calculator for each paper.
- Answer all the questions.
- Final answers should be given to a degree of accuracy appropriate to the context.
- The acceleration due to gravity is denoted by g m s^{-2}. Unless otherwise instructed, when a numerical value is needed, use $g = 9.8$.
- Show all necessary working; otherwise marks for method may be lost.
- Write your answers clearly in the spaces provided.
- Do all rough work in this book. Cross through any work that you do not want to be marked.
- You are reminded of the need for clear presentation in your answers.
- The maximum mark for each paper is 75 marks.
- The marks for questions are shown in brackets.

Paper 1

Section A: Pure Mathematics

1 The points A and B have position vectors $\mathbf{a} = \begin{bmatrix} -2 \\ 4 \end{bmatrix}$ and $\mathbf{b} = \begin{bmatrix} 5 \\ 1 \end{bmatrix}$ respectively. Point P is on the line AB such that $AP: PB = 1:3$. Find the position vector of P. [4]

....

....

....

....

....

....

....

....

....

....

....

....

2 In each of the following cases choose one of the statements.

$\text{A} \Rightarrow \text{B}, \text{A} \Leftrightarrow \text{B}, \text{A} \Leftarrow \text{B}$

(a) A: $(x-2)^2 > 0$

B: $x > 2$ [2]

....

....

....

....

(b) A: $x > 4$

B: $x^2 - 6x + 8 > 0$ [2]

....

....

....

....

(c) A: $x = 3$

B: $x^3 - 27 = 0$, where x is real. [2]

....

....

3 Differentiate from first principles.

$y = 3x^3 + 2x^2 + x + 1$ [5]

....

....

....

....

....

....

....

....

4 Consider the triangle ABC, where $AB = 8$, $BC = 6$ and $\angle CAB = 45°$.

(a) Find the two possible values of the angle at C. Give your answers to 1 decimal place. [4]

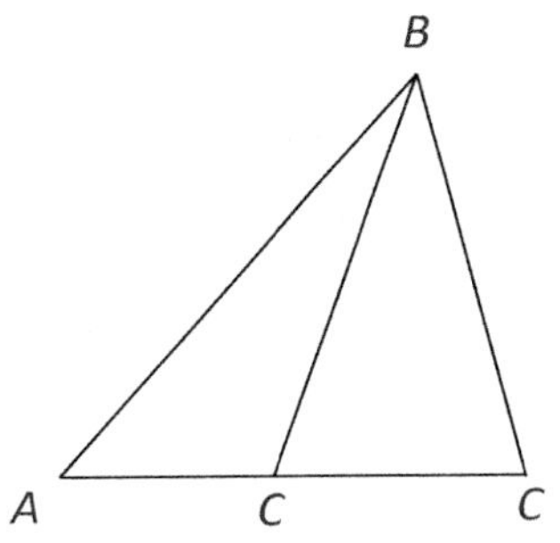

....

....

....

....

....

....

....

....

....

(b) Hence find the two possible values of the area of the triangle ABC. Give your answers to 1 decimal place. [4]

....

....

....

....

....

....

....

....

....

....

5 Two variables, x and y, are related by the equation $y = ka^x$. When $\log_2 y$ is plotted against x, a straight line passing through the points $A(0, 3)$ and $B(6, 15)$ is obtained, as shown in the diagram. Find the values of k and a. [5]

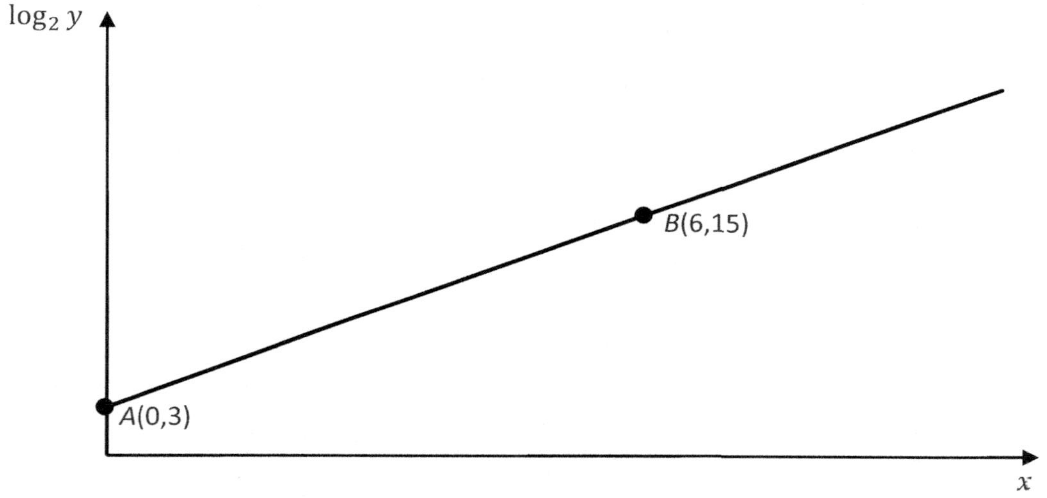

....

....

....

....

....

....

....

....

6 The sketch shows the curve of $y = f(x)$. The curve passes through the origin O and has a local maximum at $A(1, \frac{2}{3})$ and a local minimum at $B(3, 0)$.

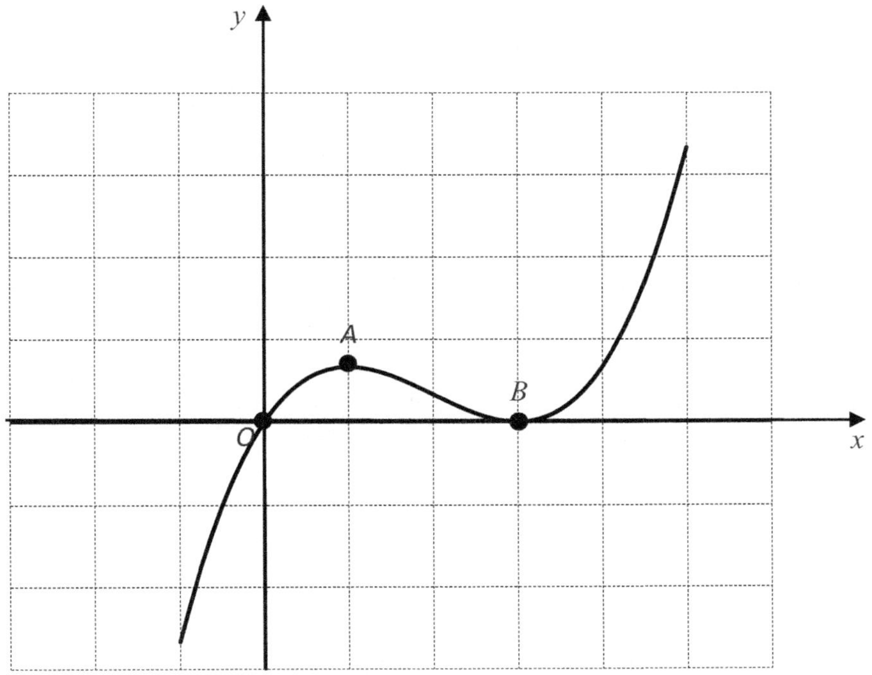

On separate diagrams, sketch the following curves, indicating clearly the coordinates of the images of the points O, A and B.

(a) $y = f(x + 1)$; [2]

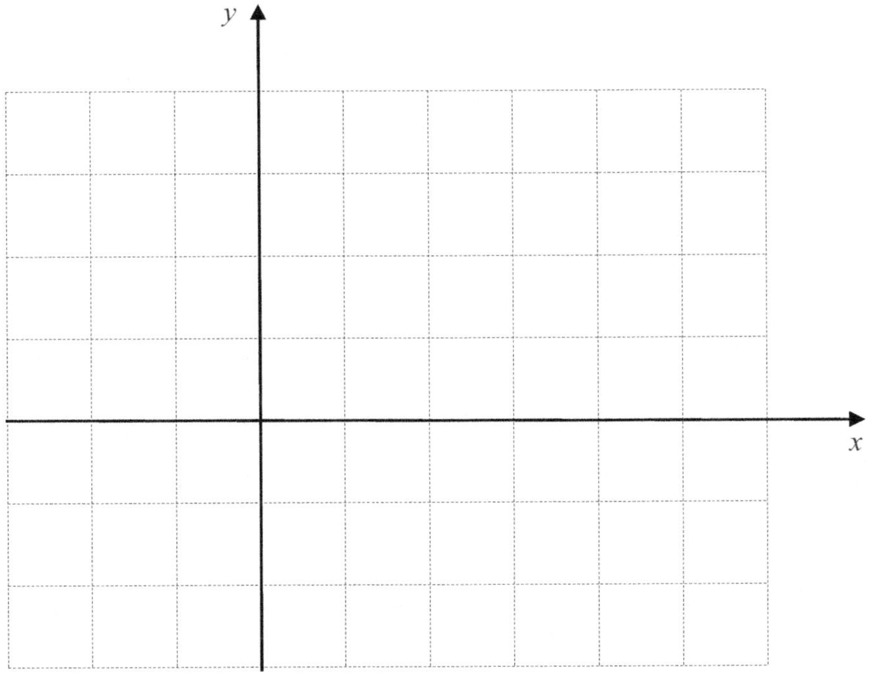

(b) $y = 2f(x)$; [2]

....

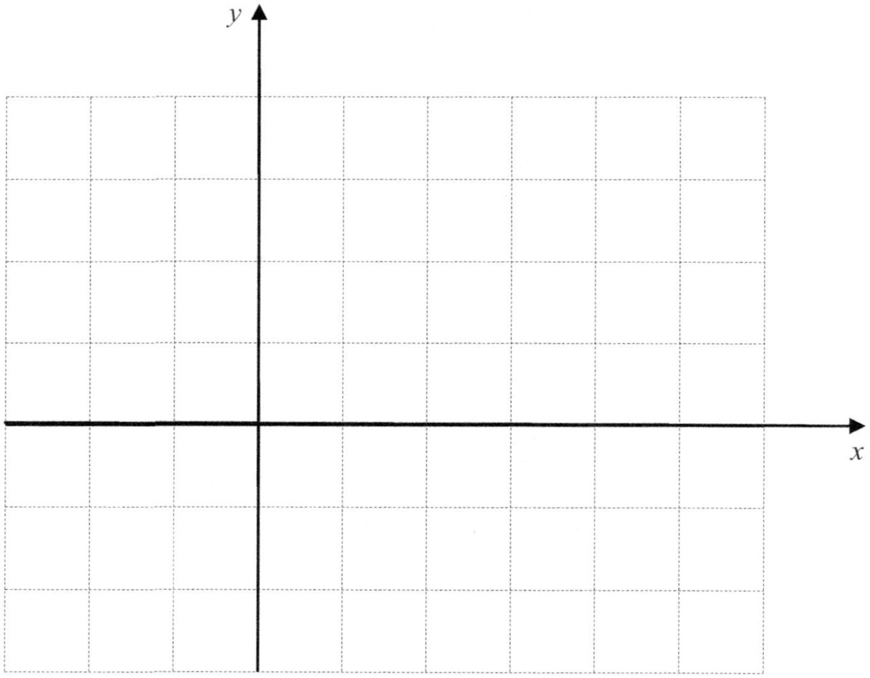

(c) $y = f(2x)$. [2]

....

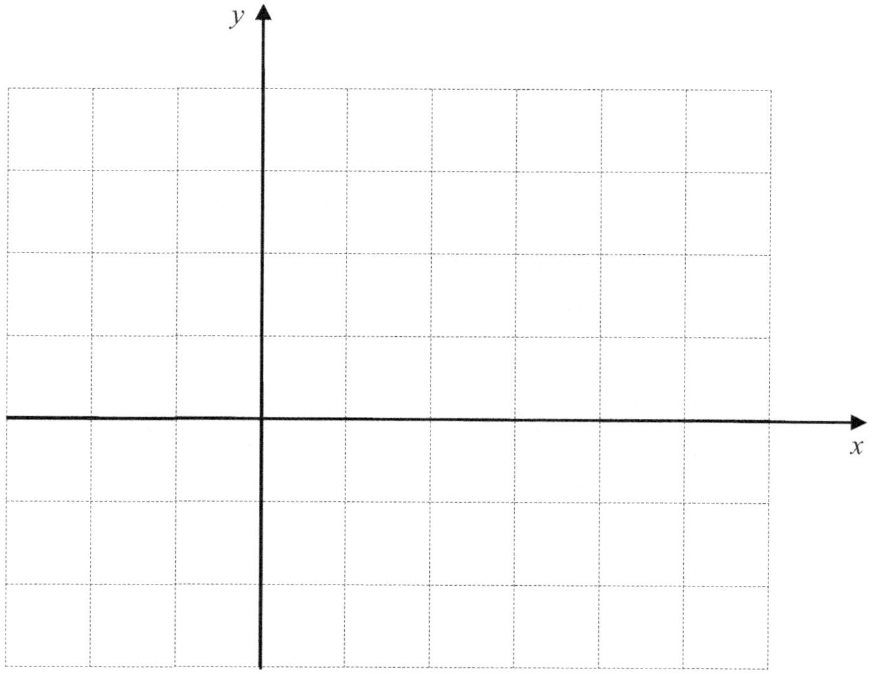

7 A circle has a chord at $A(8, 0)$ and $B(12, 4)$.

(a) Given that the centre of the circle is at $C(4, k)$, find the value of k. [5]

....

....

....

....

....

....

....

....

....

....

....

....

....

(b) Find the equation of the circle in the form $x^2 + y^2 + ax + by + c = 0$. [3]

....

....

....

....

8 A colony of bacteria is exposed to a drug that stimulates reproduction. The number of bacteria is given by the model $P = 2000 + 15t^2 - t^3$ where P is the number of bacteria present t minutes after the drug is introduced, $0 \leq t \leq 20$.

(a) Find the initial number of bacteria. [2]

....

....

(b) Find $\frac{dP}{dt}$, interpret $\frac{dP}{dt}$ in context. [2]

....

....

....

(c) Find intervals where the population of bacteria is increasing and decreasing. Justify your answer using $\frac{dP}{dt}$. [2]

....

....

....

....

....

....

(d) Comment on the long-term accuracy of the model. [2]

....

....

....

....

Section B: Mechanics

9 An object is held in equilibrium by the forces $(3\mathbf{i} - 2\mathbf{j})$N, $(-4\mathbf{i} - 4\mathbf{j})$N and **F**.

Find the force **F**. [2]

....

....

10 The graph shows the velocity of a moving carriage on a roller coaster ride.

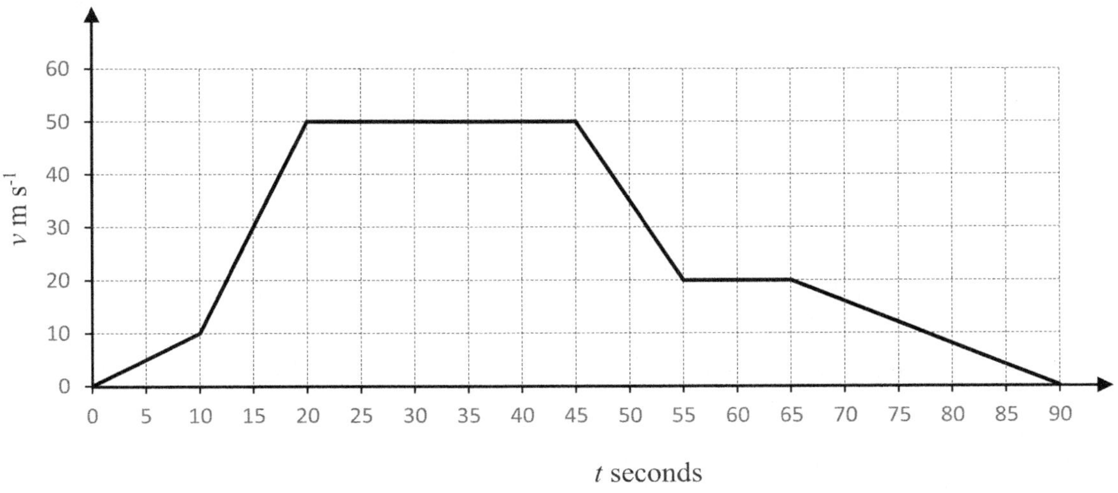

(a) Calculate the acceleration of the carriage at $t = 15$ s. [3]

....

....

....

....

(b) Jack says that the carriage travels further in the first 45 seconds of its journey than the second 45 seconds, Is Jack's statement correct? Provide evidence to support your answer. [5]

....

....

....

....

....

....

....

(c) After T seconds, the carriage has travelled 600 m. Find the value of T. [3]

....

....

....

....

....

....

....

....

....

....

11 Masses A of 0.2 kg and B of 0.4 kg are attached to the ends of a light, inextensible string which hangs over a smooth pulley as shown in the diagram. Initially B is held at rest 2 m above the ground. A rests on the ground with the string taut. Then B is let go.

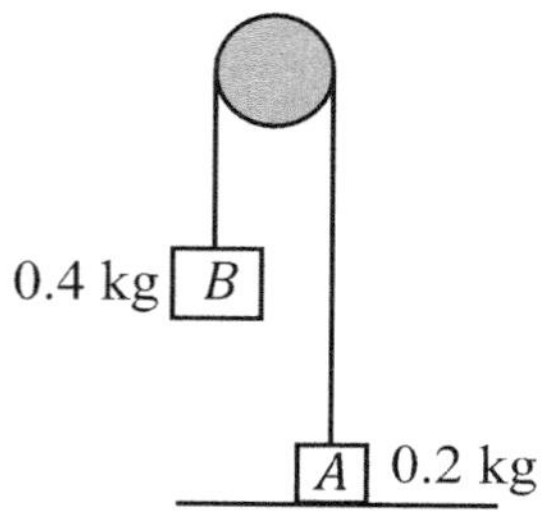

(a) Draw a diagram for each mass showing the forces acting on it and the direction of its acceleration at a later time when A and B are moving with an acceleration of a m s^{-2} and before B hits the ground. [3]

(b) Write down the equation of each mass in the direction it moves. [3]

....

....

....

(c) Use your equation to find a and the tension in the string. Give your answers to 3 significant figures. [2]

....

....

....

....

(d) Find the time taken for B to hit the ground. Give your answers to 3 significant figures. [2]

....

....

....

....

(e) State any assumptions made in your model. [2]

....

....

Paper 2

Section A: Pure Mathematics

1 Points S, T, U and V make a parallelogram, $STUV$. The position vectors of S, T and V are $\begin{bmatrix}1\\1\end{bmatrix}$, $\begin{bmatrix}8\\1\end{bmatrix}$ and $\begin{bmatrix}-2\\6\end{bmatrix}$ respectively. Find the distance between S and U. Give your answer in exact surd form. [4]

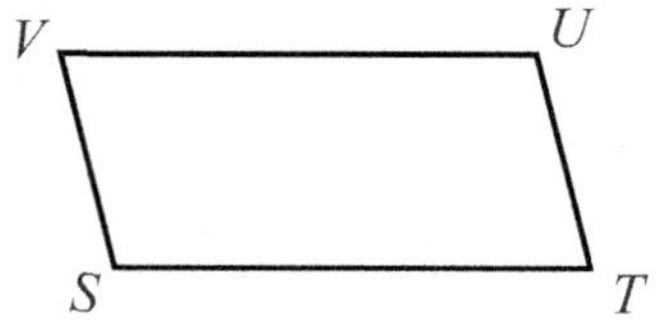

2 It is given that $(x-1)$ and $(x-2)$ are two factors of $f(x)$, where
$f(x) = x^3 - 2x^2 + px + q$

(a) Find the value of p and the value of q. [2]

(b) Fully factorise $f(x)$. [2]

3 The diagram shows triangle OAB, with $OA = 4$ cm, $OB = 6$ cm and $AB = 2\sqrt{7}$ cm.

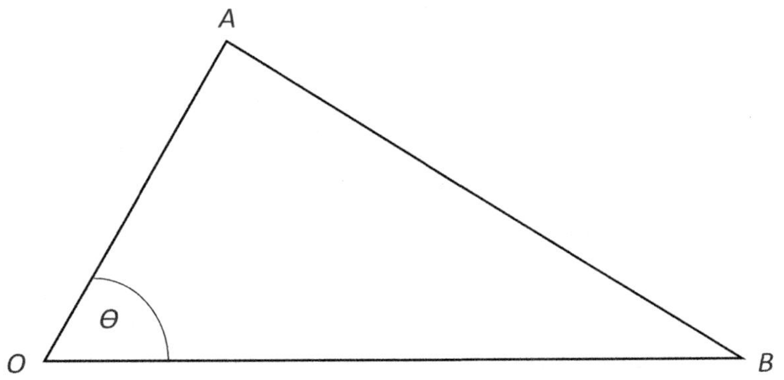

(a) Find the exact size of angle AOB. [2]

....

....

....

....

....

....

....

....

....

....

....

(b) Find the area of triangle OAB. [2]

....

....

....

....

....

....

....

....

....

....

4 Point C has coordinates $(c, 2)$ and point D has coordinates $(6, d)$. The line $y + 4x = 11$ is the perpendicular bisector of CD.

Find c and d. [4]

....

....

....

....

....

....

....

....

....

....

....

....

....

....

....

5 The graph of the equation $y = \frac{2}{x}$ is translated by the vector $\begin{bmatrix} 3 \\ 2 \end{bmatrix}$

(a) Write down the equation of the transformed graph. [2]

....

....

(b) State the equation of the asymptotes of the transformed graph. [4]

....

....

....

....

....

....

....

....

6 (a) Sketch the curve $y = (x - a)^2(3 - x)$, where $0 < a < 3$, indicating the coordinates of the points where the curve and the axes meet. [6]

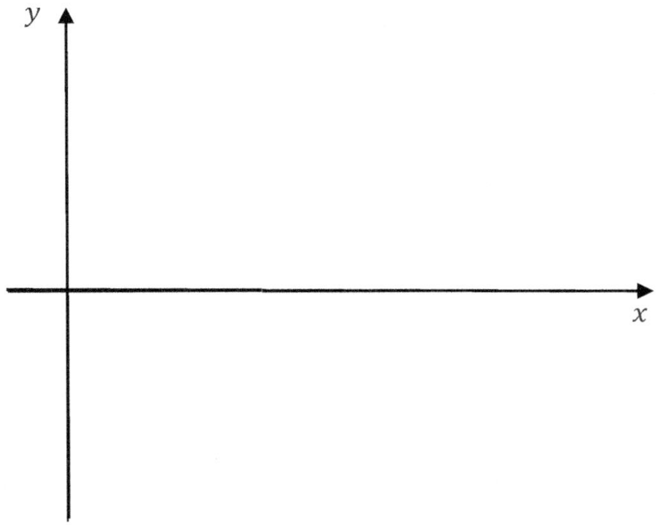

(b) Hence, solve $(x - a)^2(3 - x) > 0$, giving your answer in set notation form. [2]

7 The number of employees, p, working for a company t years after it was founded can be modelled by the equation $p = at^b$. The table below shows the number of employees the company has:

Age of company (t years)	3	6	9	12	15
Number of employees (p)	4	8	10	14	16

(a) Show that $p = at^b$ can be written in the form $\log_{10} p = b \log_{10} t + \log_{10} a$. [4]

(b) Plot a graph of $\log_{10} p$ against $\log_{10} t$ and draw a line of best fit for your graph. [4]

$\log_{10} t$					
$\log_{10} p$					

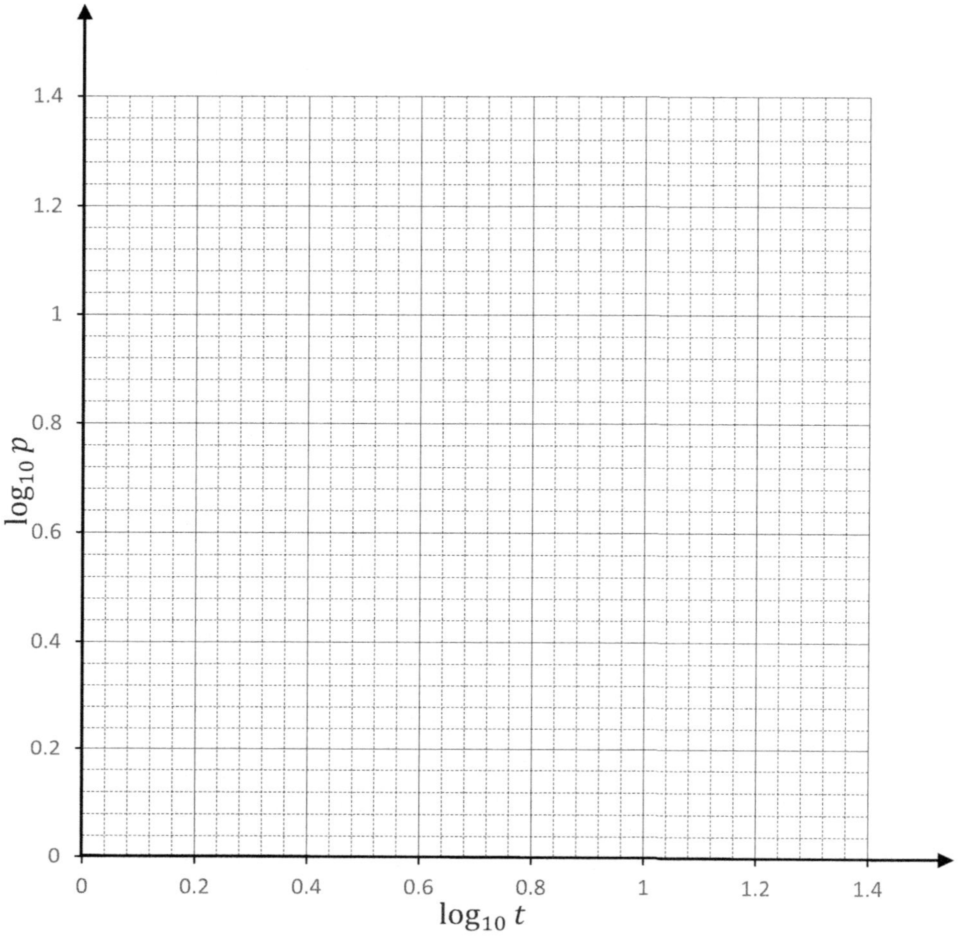

(c) Use your graph to estimate the values of a and b in the equation $p = at^b$. Give your answer to 3 decimal places. [4]

....

....

....

....

....

....

....

....

....

8 A quadratic function $f(x)$ is defined on $\mathbb{R}$. The turning point is (2, 2).

$h(x) = af(x+b) + c$, and the turning point is (7, -8). The diagram shows the graphs with equations $y = f(x)$ and $y = h(x)$.

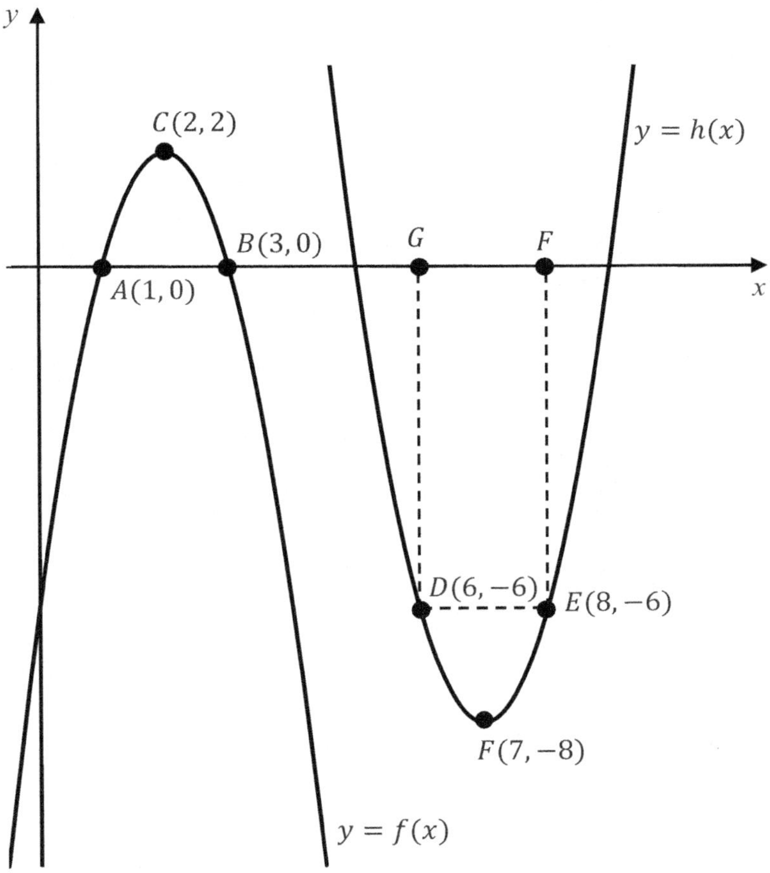

(a) Find the values of a, b and c. [4]

....

....

....

....

....

....

....

....

....

....

....

....

(b) It is known that $\int_1^3 f(x)\mathrm{d}x = \frac{8}{3}$. Find the value of $\int_6^8 h(x)\mathrm{d}x$. [4]

....

....

....

....

Section B: Mechanics

9 (a) The movement of a particle is modelled by vector **p**. The particle is travelling at a speed of 6 m s^{-1} with direction of 30° above the horizontal. Write the vector **p** in the form of $a\mathbf{i} + b\mathbf{j}$, where $a, b \in \mathbb{R}$. [2]

....

....

(b) The particle strikes another particle. Its movement is now modelled by vector $\mathbf{q} = 2\sqrt{2}(\mathbf{i} + \mathbf{j})$.

Find the amount by which the particle's speed has decreased, and state the particle's new direction. [3]

....

....

....

....

....

....

....

....

10 An ice skater of mass 55 kg is initially moving with speed 2 m s^{-1} and glides to a halt over a distance of 10 m. Assuming that the force of resistance is constant, find

(a) the value of the resistance force [3]

....

....

....

....

....

(b) the distance he would travel gliding to rest from an initial speed of 8 m s^{-1}. [2]

....

....

....

(c) the force he would need to apply to maintain a steady speed of 10 m s^{-1}. [2]

....

....

11 The diagram shows a block of mass 5 kg lying on a smooth table. It is attached to a block of mass 3 kg by a string which passes over a smooth pulley. The tension in the string is T, as shown, and the block has acceleration a m s^{-2}.

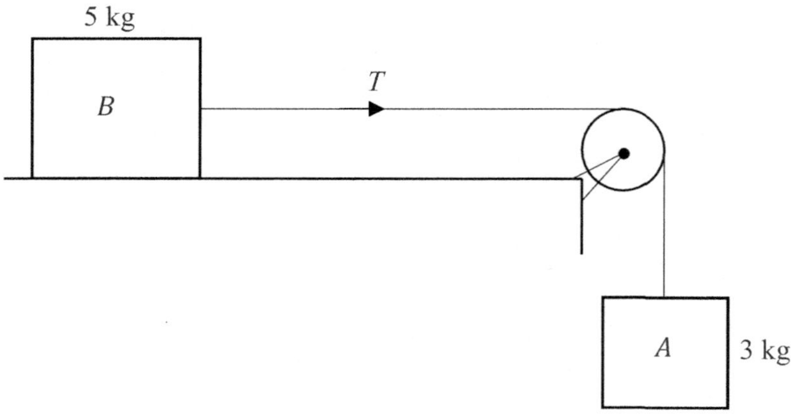

(a) Draw a diagram for each block, showing all the forces acting on it. [4]

(b) Write down the equation of motion for each of the blocks. [2]

....

....

(c) Use your equation to find the values of a and T. Give your answers to 3 significant figures. [4]

....

....

....

....

....

....

(d) In practice, the table is not truly smooth and a is found to be 2.5 m s^{-2}. Use your new equations to find the frictional force that would produce this result.

[3]

....

....

....

....

Paper 3

Section A: Pure Mathematics

1 The coefficient of x^2 in the binomial expansion of $(1 + 3x)^n$ where $n > 0$ is 495.

Find the value of n. [3]

....

....

....

....

....

2 *ABCD* is a kite where *A* is the point (1, -2), *B* is the point (7, 1) and *C* is the point (3, 4). *AC* perpendicularly bisects *BD*.

(a) Find the equation of the line *AC* in the form $y = mx + c$. [2]

....

....

....

....

....

....

(b) Find the coordinates of point *D*. [4]

....

....

....

....

....

....

....

....

....

....

....

....

....

....

....

....

....

....

....

....

(c) Find the area of the kite. [2]

....

....

....

....

3 (a) Show that the equation $9\cos\theta + \sin\theta\tan\theta - 6 = 0$ can be expressed as the equation $(2\cos\theta - 1)(4\cos\theta - 1) = 0$ [2]

....

....

....

....

....

....

(b) Find all the values of θ that solve the equation

$9\cos\theta + \sin\theta\tan\theta - 6 = 0$

for $-180° \leq \theta \leq 180°$

Give your answer to the nearest degree. [2]

....

....

....

....

....

(c) Hence, find all the solutions of the equation

$$9\cos\frac{\theta}{2} + \sin\frac{\theta}{2}\tan\frac{\theta}{2} - 6 = 0$$

for $-180° \leq \theta \leq 180°$

Give your answer to the nearest degree. [2]

....

....

....

....

....

....

4 In this question you must show detailed reasoning.

A curve has equation

$$y = \frac{a}{\sqrt{x}} + bx^2 + \frac{c}{x^3}$$

where $x > 0$, a, b and c are positive constants.

The curve has a single turning point.

Use the second derivative of y to determine the nature of this turning point.

You do not need to find the coordinates of the turning point. [6]

....

....

....

....

....

....

....

....

....

....

....

....

....

....

5 Curve C has equation $y = x^2$, C is translated by vector $\begin{bmatrix} 3 \\ 0 \end{bmatrix}$ to give curve C_1.

Line L has equation $y = x$, L is stretched by scale factor 2 parallel to the x-axis to give line L_1.

Find the exact distance between the two intersection points of C_1 and L_1 [5]

....

....

....

....

....

....

....

....

....

....

....

....

....

....

6 A circle has equation $x^2 + y^2 + 10x - 4y - 71 = 0$

(a) Find the centre of the circle. [2]

....

....

(b) Hence, find the equation of the tangent to the circle at the point (1, 10), giving your answer in the form $ax + bx + c = 0$, where a, b and c are integers. [3]

....

....

....

....

....

....

....

7 (a) Find

$$\int (4x - x^3)\mathrm{d}x$$ [2]

(b) Evaluate

$$\int_{-2}^{2} (4x - x^3)\mathrm{d}x$$ [2]

(c) Using a sketch, explain why the integral in part (b) does not give the area enclosed between the curve $y = 4x - x^3$ and the x-axis. [3]

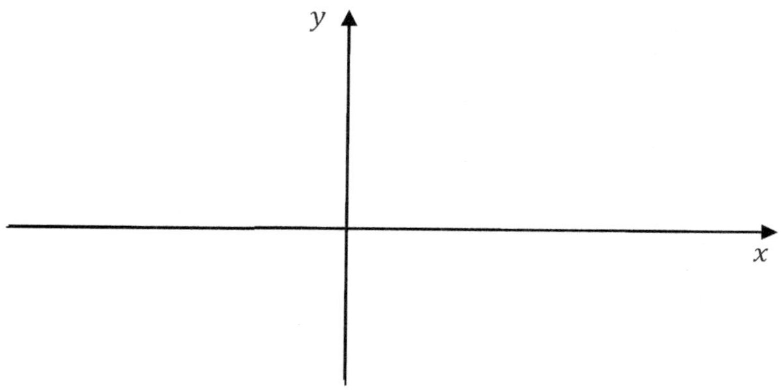

(d) Find the area enclosed between the curve $y = 4x - x^3$ and the x-axis. [2]

Area is:

8 The yearly income from book sales of a particular author has tended to increase with time. The table below shows his income from book sales over the first five years after his book was published.

Number of years after book published (t)	1	2	3	4	5
Income (£p thousand)	10	13	17	24	35

The relationship is modelled by the equation $p = ab^t$, where a and b are constants to be found.

(a) Plot a graph of $\log_{10} p$ against t and draw a line of best fit for your graph. [3]

t					
$\log_{10} p$					

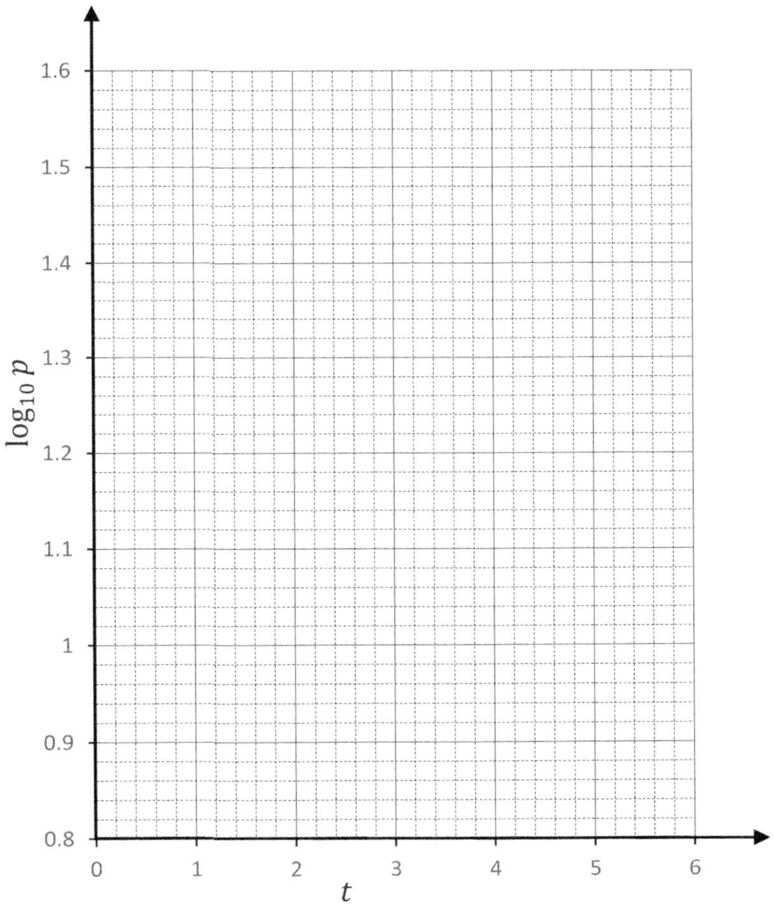

(b) State, in terms of a and b, the gradient and vertical-axis intercept of your graph.

Hence use your graph to find the values of a and b. Give your answers to 3 significant figures. [3]

....

....

....

....

....

....

....

....

....

....

....

....

(c) Predict the author's income 10 years after his book was published. [1]

....

....

(d) Suggest one reason why the prediction in part (c) might not be accurate. [1]

....

....

Section B: Mechanics

9 Two forces, $(x\mathbf{i} + y\mathbf{j})$N and $(5\mathbf{i} + \mathbf{j})$N, act on a particle P of mass 2.5 kg. The resultant of the two forces is $(8\mathbf{i} - 3\mathbf{j})$N. Find

(a) the values of x and y. [2]

....

....

....

....

....

....

(b) the magnitude and direction of the acceleration of P, giving your answers to 3 significant figures. [3]

....

....

....

....

....

....

....

....

....

....

(c) the particle's velocity vector, 5 seconds after it accelerates from rest. [2]

....

....

....

....

....

....

....

....

10 A particle sets off from the origin O at $t = 0$ s and moves in a straight line. At time t seconds, the velocity of the particle is v m s^{-1}, where

$$v = \begin{cases} 9t - 3t^2 & 0 \leq t \leq 2 \text{ s} \\ \dfrac{24}{t^2} & t > 2 \text{ s} \end{cases}$$

(a) Sketch the graph of the velocity of the particle against time. [3]

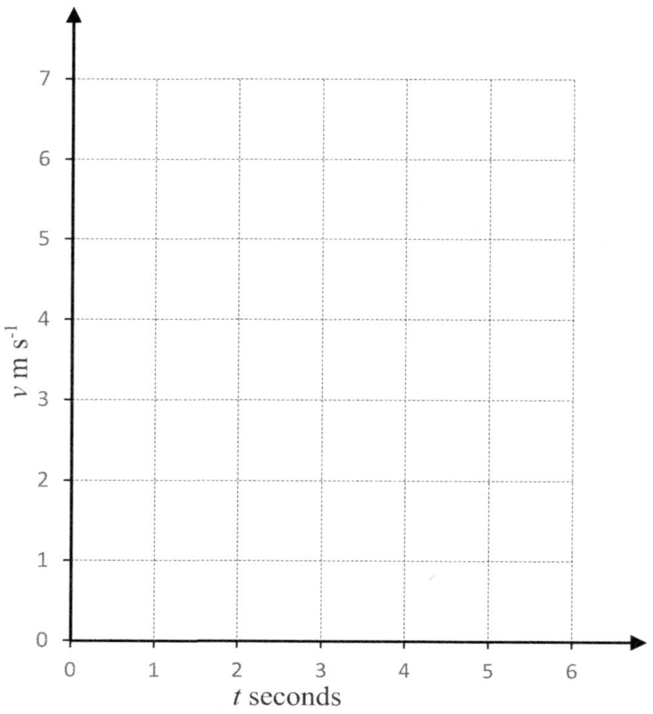

(b) Find the maximum speed of the particle in the interval $0 \leq t \leq 2$ s [3]

....

....

....

....

(c) Find the displacement of the particle from O at

(i) $t = 2$ s [2]

....

....

(ii) $t = 6$ s [2]

....

....

11 The diagram shows two particles, A and B. A is of mass $3m$ kg and rests on a rough plane with coefficient of friction 0.25. A is connected to B by a light inextensible string which passes over a smooth pulley. B is of mass $2m$ kg and hangs freely. The system is released from rest with the string taut.

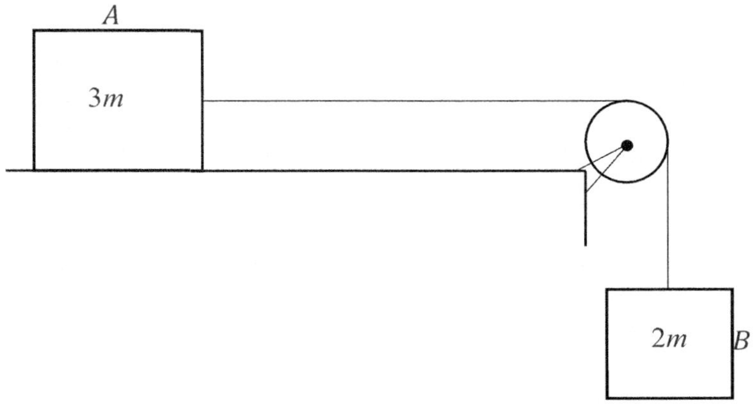

(a) Find the initial acceleration of the system in terms of g. [2]

....

....

....

....

....

....

....

....

....

....

....

....

....

....

....

....

....

....

....

(b) The system is release with B 1 m above the ground. When B hits the ground, the string goes slack. Find the total distance moved by A before coming to rest again, assuming that it does not hit the pulley. [4]

....

....

....

....

....

....

....

....

....

....

....

....

....

(c) State where you have used the assumption that the pulley is smooth. [2]

....

....

Paper 4

Section A: Pure Mathematics

1 It is given that $\cos\ 15° = \dfrac{\sqrt{3}+1}{2\sqrt{2}}$, $\sin 15° = \dfrac{\sqrt{3}-1}{2\sqrt{2}}$

Find the exact value of tan 15°, giving your answer in the form $a - \sqrt{b}\ , a, b \in \mathbb{Z}^{+}$.

[3]

....

....

2 (a) Using $y = 2^{2x}$ as a substitution, show that

$16^{x} - 2^{(2x+3)} - 9 = 0$ can be written as $y^{2} - 8y - 9 = 0$ [2]

....

....

(b) Hence, solve the equation $16^{x} - 2^{(2x+3)} - 9 = 0$, giving the exact value of x.

[3]

....

....

....

....

3 (a) Express $2x^{2} - 8x + k$ in the form $a(x-b)^{2} + c$ [2]

....

....

(b) Find the value of k for which the curve $y = 2x^{2} - 8x + k$ does not intersect the line $y = 4$ [3]

....

....

....

....

....

....

4 (a) Show that $\sin\theta = 1$ is one solution of the equation

$$5\cos^2\theta + 6\sin\theta = 6$$ [2]

....

....

....

....

(b) Find all the values of θ that solve the equation

$$5\cos^2\theta + 6\sin\theta = 6$$

for $0° \leq \theta \leq 360°$

Give your answer to the nearest degree. [3]

....

....

....

....

(c) Hence, find all the solutions of the equation

$$5\cos^2 2\theta + 6\sin 2\theta = 6$$

for $0° \leq \theta \leq 360°$

Give your answer to the nearest degree. [3]

....

....

....

....

5 For each of the following statements, decide whether it is true or false. If true, give a proof; if false, give a counterexample.

(a) If n is any positive integer, then $2^n - 1$ is prime. [2]

....

....

....

....

....

(b) If the sum of the digits of a four-digit number is divisible by 3, then the four-digit number is also divisible by 3. [5]

....

....

....

....

....

....

....

....

....

....

....

....

6 The diagram shows a sector AOB of a circle with centre O and radius r cm.

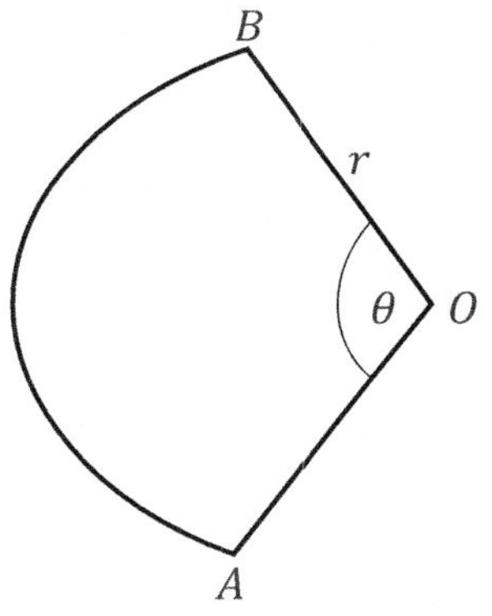

The angle AOB is θ radians. The sector has perimeter 30 cm.

(a) Find the area of the sector in terms of r. [3]

....

....

....

....

....

....

....

....

(b) Use calculus to find the value of r which maximises the area, and calculate the area and the angle AOB. [4]

....

....

....

....

....

....

....

....

7 The diagram shows the graphs with equations $y = f(x)$ and $y = bf(x) + a$.

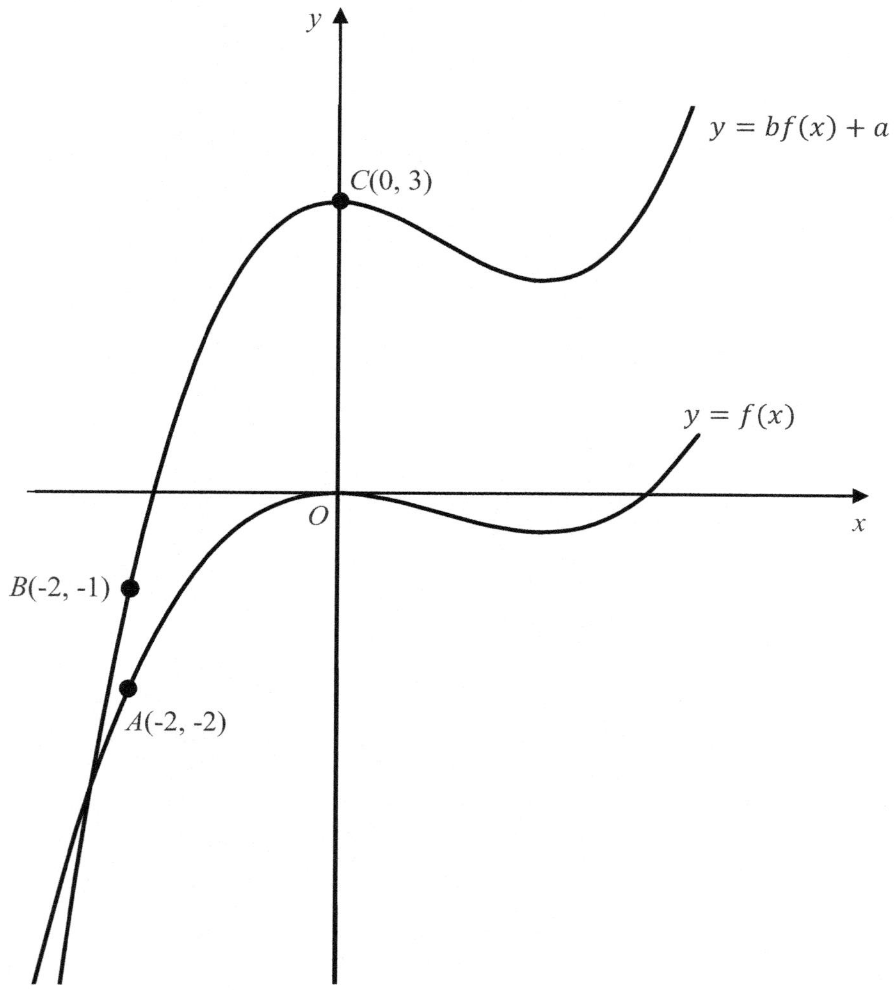

(a) Find the value of a. [4]

....

....

....

....

(b) Find the value of b. [4]

....

....

....

....

8 Susan is baking a birthday cake. She places the cake mix in a preheated oven. The temperature in the centre of the cake mix in °C is modelled by the function $H(t) = 180 - a(1.08)^{-t}$ where the time t is in minutes after the mix is placed in the oven, The graph of $H(t)$ is given.

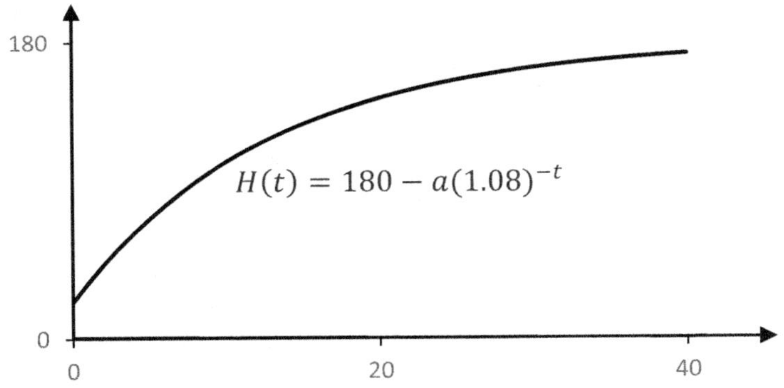

(a) Write down what the value of 180 represents in the context of the question.[2]

....

....

....

(b) The temperature in the centre of the cake mix was 22°C when placed in the oven. Find the value of a. [2]

....

....

....

(c) The cake is removed from the oven 29 minutes after the temperature in the centre of the cake has reached 150°C.

Find the total time that the baking tin is the oven. Give your answers to 3 significant figures. [3]

....

....

....

....

....

....

Section B: Mechanics

9 A wooden crate rests on a rough horizontal surface. The coefficient of friction between the crate and the surface is 0.8. A boy attempts to move a wooden crate. When he applied a horizontal force of 150 N, the crate is on the point of moving.

(a) Find the mass of the crate. Give your answer to 3 decimal places. [2]

....

....

....

....

(b) Instead, the boy use a handle to pull the crate forward. He exerts a force of 150 N, at an angle of $30°$ above the horizontal, as shown in the diagram. What acceleration must the boy have in order to do this? Give your answer to 3 decimal places. [3]

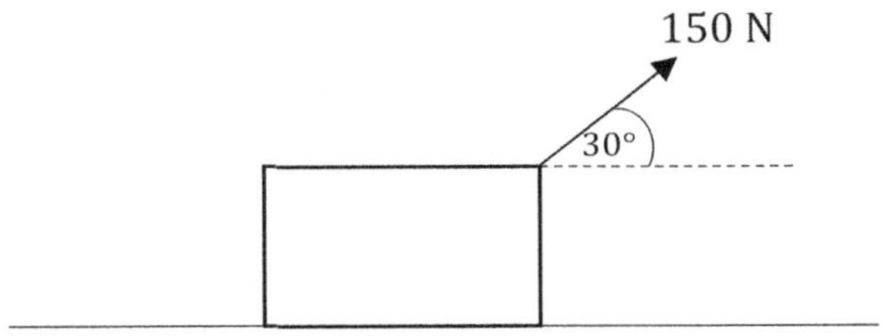

....

....

....

....

....

....

....

....

....

....

....

....

....

....

10 The height, h metres, of an object that is moving along a vertical path is given by the function $h = 112 + 96t - 16t^2$, where t is the time, in seconds.

(a) Find the maximum height of the object and the time at which it reaches maximum height. [3]

....

....

....

....

....

....

(b) Find the object's velocity when its height is 0 metre. [3]

....

....

....

....

....

....

....

....

11 A woman of mass 60 kg is standing in a lift and the lift has a mass of 340 kg. Find the tension in the cable supporting the lift and the force exerted on the woman by the lift by when

(a) the lift is at rest [4]

....

....

....

....

....

....

....

....

(b) the lift is moving at constant speed [2]

....

....

....

....

....

....

(c) the lift is accelerating upwards at 0.9 m s^{-2} [4]

....

....

....

....

(d) the lift is accelerating downwards at 0.5 m s^{-2}. [4]

....

....

....

....

....

....

Paper 1 solutions

Section A: Pure Mathematics

1 The points A and B have position vectors $\mathbf{a} = \begin{bmatrix} -2 \\ 4 \end{bmatrix}$ and $\mathbf{b} = \begin{bmatrix} 5 \\ 1 \end{bmatrix}$ respectively. Point P is on the line AB such that $AP: PB = 1: 3$. Find the position vector of P. [4]

$\overrightarrow{AB} = \overrightarrow{OB} - \overrightarrow{OA} = \begin{bmatrix} 5 \\ 1 \end{bmatrix} - \begin{bmatrix} -2 \\ 4 \end{bmatrix} = \begin{bmatrix} 7 \\ -3 \end{bmatrix}$

P is $\dfrac{1}{4}$ of the way along $\overrightarrow{AB}$, so we have

$$\overrightarrow{AP} = \frac{1}{4}\overrightarrow{AB} = \frac{\begin{bmatrix} 7 \\ -3 \end{bmatrix}}{4} = \begin{bmatrix} \frac{7}{4} \\ -\frac{3}{4} \end{bmatrix}$$

$$\overrightarrow{OP} = \overrightarrow{OA} + \overrightarrow{AP} = \begin{bmatrix} -2 \\ 4 \end{bmatrix} + \begin{bmatrix} \frac{7}{4} \\ -\frac{3}{4} \end{bmatrix} = \begin{bmatrix} -\frac{1}{4} \\ \frac{13}{4} \end{bmatrix}$$

The position vector of P is

$$\begin{bmatrix} -\frac{1}{4} \\ \frac{13}{4} \end{bmatrix}$$

2 In each of the following cases choose one of the statements.

$\mathrm{A} \Rightarrow \mathrm{B}, \mathrm{A} \Leftrightarrow \mathrm{B}, \mathrm{A} \Leftarrow \mathrm{B}$

(a) A: $(x - 2)^2 > 0$

B: $x > 2$ [2]

$(x - 2)^2 > 0 \Rightarrow x > 2 \text{ or } x < 2$

$x > 2 \Rightarrow (x - 2)^2 > 0$

Therefore $\mathrm{A} \Leftarrow \mathrm{B}$

(b) A: $x > 4$

B: $x^2 - 6x + 8 > 0$ [2]

$x^2 - 6x + 8 > 0 \Rightarrow (x - 2)(x - 4) > 0 \Rightarrow x > 4 \text{ or } x < 2$

$x > 4 \Rightarrow (x - 2)(x - 4) > 0, x^2 - 6x + 8 > 0$

Therefore $\mathrm{A} \Rightarrow \mathrm{B}$

(c) A: $x = 3$

B: $x^3 - 27 = 0$, where x is real. [2]

$x^3 - 27 = 0 \Rightarrow x = 3 \Rightarrow x^3 - 27 = 0$

Therefore A $\Leftrightarrow$ B

3 Differentiate from first principles.

$y = 3x^3 + 2x^2 + x + 1$ [5]

$$\lim_{h\to 0}\frac{3(x+h)^3 + 2(x+h)^2 + (x+h) + 1 - (3x^3 + 2x^2 + x + 1)}{h}$$

$$= \lim_{h\to 0}\frac{9x^2h + 9xh^2 + 3h^3 + 4xh + 2h^2 + h}{h}$$

$$= \lim_{h\to 0}(9x^2 + 9xh + 3h^2 + 4x + 2h + 1) = 9x^2 + 4x + 1 \Rightarrow$$

$$\frac{\mathrm{d}y}{\mathrm{d}x} = 9x^2 + 4x + 1$$

4 Consider the triangle ABC, where $AB = 8$, $BC = 6$ and $\angle CAB = 45°$.

(a) Find the two possible values of the angle at C. Give your answers to 1 decimal place. [4]

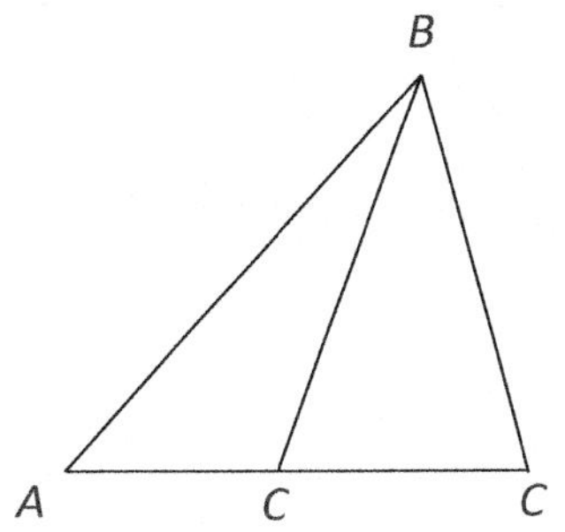

$$\frac{\sin 45°}{6} = \frac{\sin\angle ACB}{8}, \sin\angle ACB = \frac{2\sqrt{2}}{3}$$

$\angle ACB = 70.5°$

and

$\angle ACB = 180° - 70.5° = 109.5°$

(b) Hence find the two possible values of the area of the triangle ABC. Give your answers to 1 decimal place. [4]

$\angle ABC = 180° - \angle ACB - \angle BAC = 180° - 70.5° - 45° = 64.5°$

and $\angle ABC = 180° - \angle ACB - \angle BAC = 180° - 109.5° - 45° = 25.5°$

The area of the triangle ABC is

$$\frac{1}{2}AB \times BC \times \sin\angle ABC = \frac{1}{2} \times 8 \times 6 \times \sin 64.5° = 21.7$$

Or

$$\frac{1}{2}AB \times BC \times \sin\angle ABC = \frac{1}{2} \times 8 \times 6 \times \sin 25.5° = 10.3$$

5 Two variables, x and y, are related by the equation $y = ka^x$. When $\log_2 y$ is plotted against x, a straight line passing through the points $A(0, 3)$ and $B(6, 15)$ is obtained, as shown in the diagram. Find the values of k and a. [5]

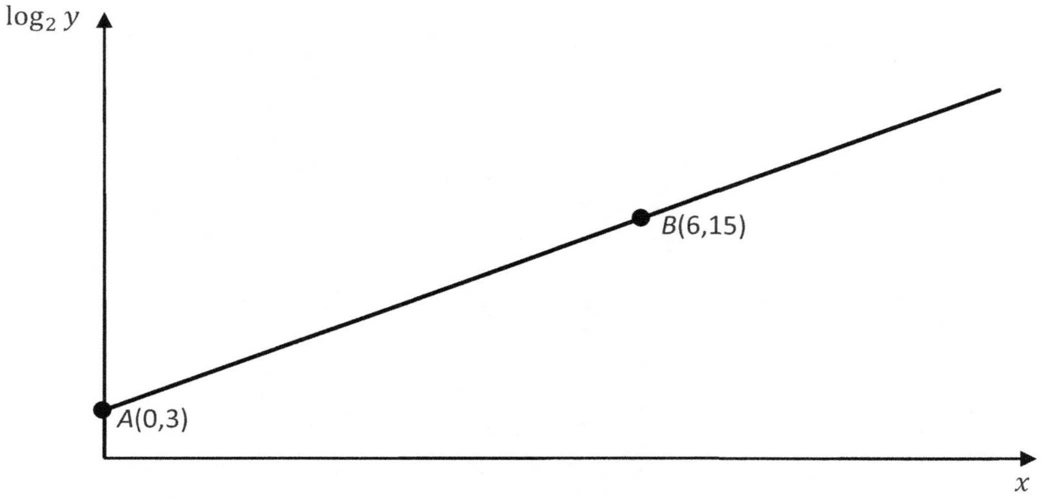

$y = ka^x \Rightarrow \log_2 y = x \log_2 a + \log_2 k$

$\log_2 a$ is the gradient of the line. $\log_2 k$ is the vertical-axis intercept of the line.

Therefore we have:

$$\log_2 a = \frac{15 - 3}{6 - 0} = 2 \Rightarrow a = 2^2 = 4$$

$$\log_2 k = 3 \Rightarrow k = 2^3 = 8$$

$$a = 4, k = 8$$

6 The sketch shows the curve of $y = f(x)$. The curve passes through the origin O and has a local maximum at $A(1, \frac{2}{3})$ and a local minimum at $B(3, 0)$.

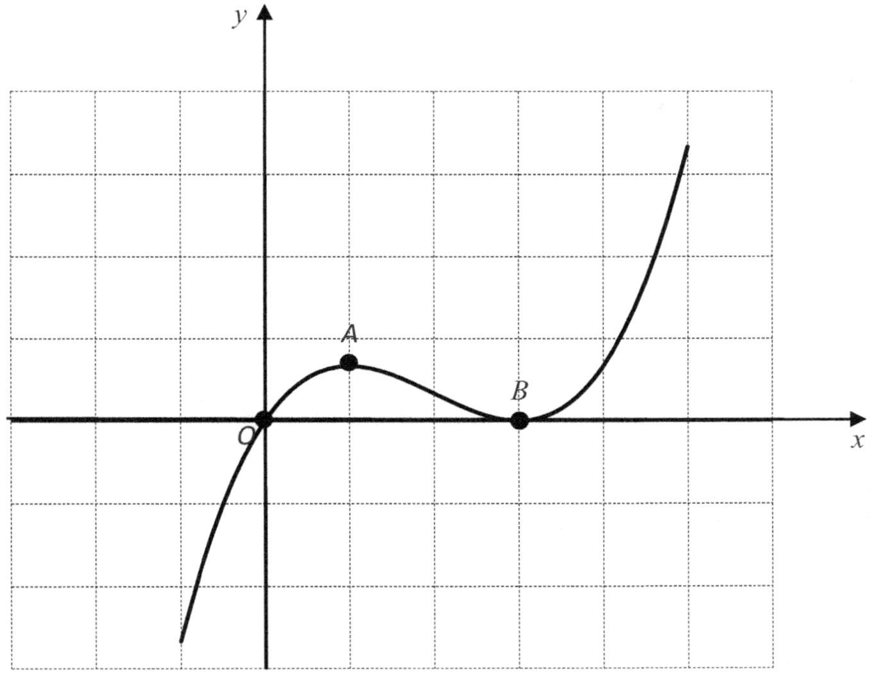

On separate diagrams, sketch the following curves, indicating clearly the coordinates of the images of the points O, A and B.

(a) $y = f(x + 1)$; [2]

Horizontal translation, 1 unit in the negative x-direction.

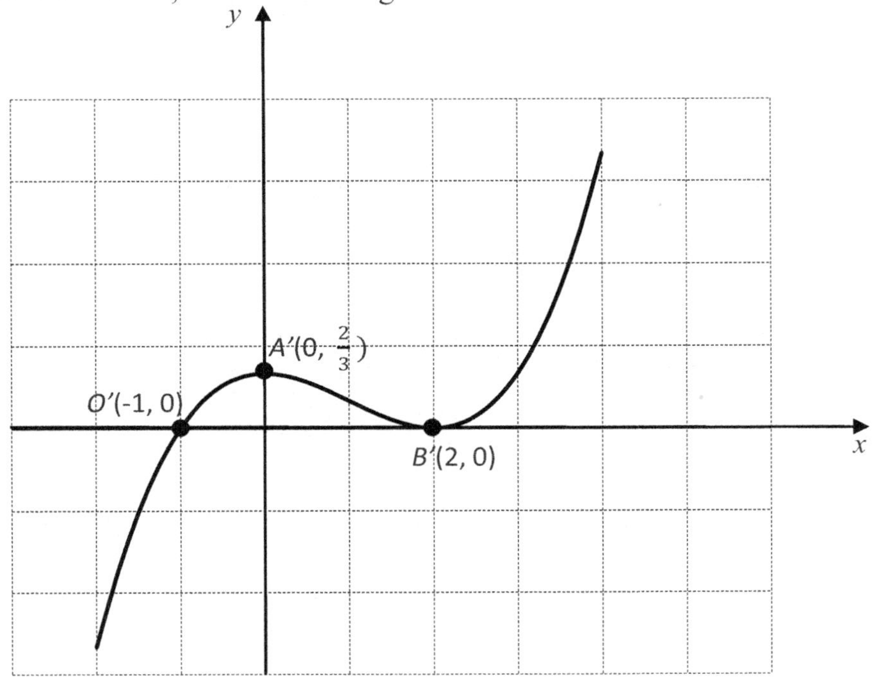

(b) $y = 2f(x)$; [2]

Stretch in the y-direction.

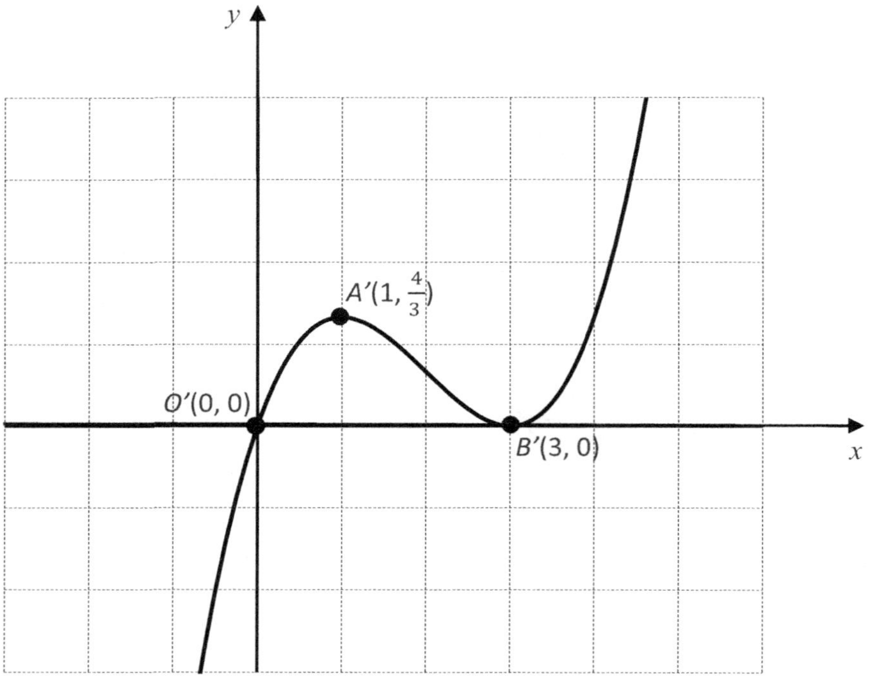

(c) $y = f(2x)$. [2]

Horizontal stretch with scale factor 0.5.

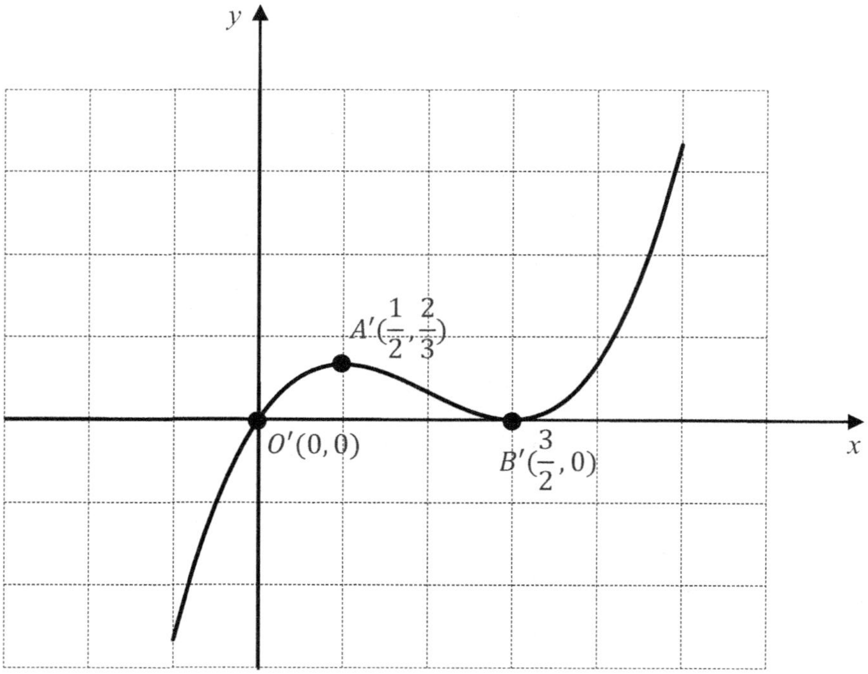

7 A circle has a chord at $A(8, 0)$ and $B(12, 4)$.

(a) Given that the centre of the circle is at $C(4, k)$, find the value of k. [5]

The midpoint of A and B is

$$\left(\frac{8+12}{2}, \frac{0+4}{2}\right) \Rightarrow (10, 2)$$

The gradient of AB is

$$\frac{4-0}{12-8} = 1$$

The gradient of the perpendicular bisector of AB is -1

The equation of the perpendicular bisector of AB can be obtained by

$$y - 2 = -(x - 10) \Rightarrow y = -x + 12$$

The centre of the circle lies on the perpendicular bisector of AB.

$$y = -4 + 12 = 8 \Rightarrow k = 8$$

(b) Find the equation of the circle in the form $x^2 + y^2 + ax + by + c = 0$. [3]

The radius of the circle can be calculated by using the points A and C.

$$r = \sqrt{(8-4)^2 + (0-8)^2} = \sqrt{80}$$

The equation of the circle can be obtained by

$$(x-4)^2 + (y-8)^2 = 80 \Rightarrow x^2 + y^2 - 8x - 16y = 0$$

8 A colony of bacteria is exposed to a drug that stimulates reproduction. The number of bacteria is given by the model $P = 2000 + 15t^2 - t^3$ where P is the number of bacteria present t minutes after the drug is introduced, $0 \leq t \leq 20$.

(a) Find the initial number of bacteria. [2]

When $t = 0$, $P = 2000$

(b) Find $\frac{dP}{dt}$, interpret $\frac{dP}{dt}$ in context. [2]

$$\frac{dP}{dt} = 30t - 3t^2$$

It is the rate of change of number of bacteria.

(c) Find intervals where the population of bacteria is increasing and decreasing. Justify your answer using $\frac{\mathrm{d}P}{\mathrm{d}t}$. [2]

$$\frac{\mathrm{d}P}{\mathrm{d}t} = 30t - 3t^2 = 3t(10 - t)$$

For $0 < t < 10$, $\frac{\mathrm{d}P}{\mathrm{d}t} > 0 \Rightarrow$ The population of bacteria is increasing.

For $10 < \mathrm{t} < 20$, $\frac{\mathrm{d}P}{\mathrm{d}t} < 0 \Rightarrow$ The population of bacteria is decreasing.

(d) Comment on the long-term accuracy of the model. [2]

Eventually all of the bacteria will die so the model will no longer be accurate.

Section B: Mechanics

9 An object is held in equilibrium by the forces $(3\mathbf{i} - 2\mathbf{j})$N, $(-4\mathbf{i} - 4\mathbf{j})$N and $\mathbf{F}$.

Find the force $\mathbf{F}$. [2]

$(3\mathbf{i} - 2\mathbf{j}) + (-4\mathbf{i} - 4\mathbf{j}) + \mathbf{F} = \mathbf{0} \Rightarrow$

$\mathbf{F} = -(3\mathbf{i} - 2\mathbf{j}) - (-4\mathbf{i} - 4\mathbf{j}) = (\mathbf{i} + 6\mathbf{j})$N

10 The graph shows the velocity of a moving carriage on a roller coaster ride.

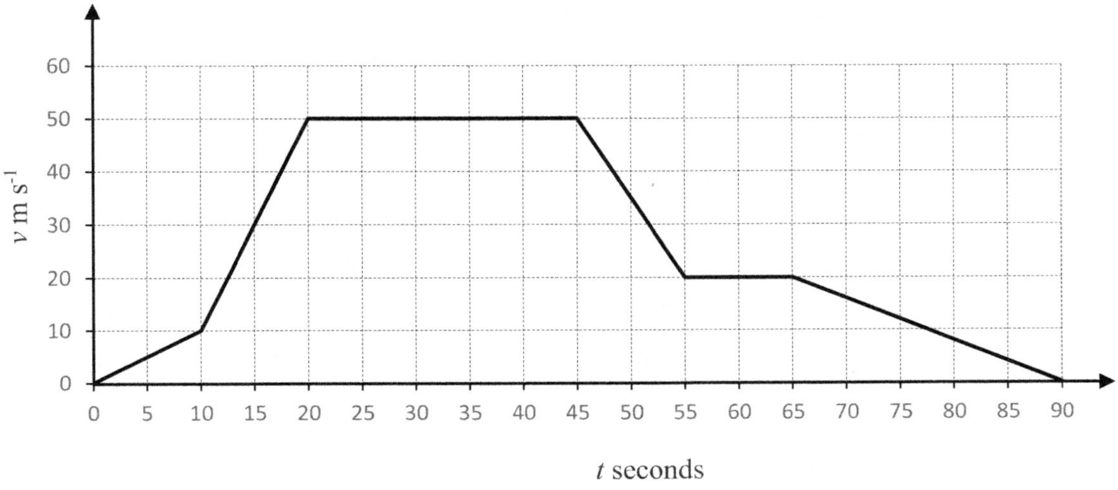

(a) Calculate the acceleration of the carriage at $t = 15$ s. [3]

Acceleration is the gradient of the graph. The two points (10, 10) and (20, 50) can be used to calculate the gradient at $t = 15$ s.

$$a = \frac{50 - 10}{20 - 10} = 4 \text{ m s}^{-2}$$

(b) Jack says that the carriage travels further in the first 45 seconds of its journey than the second 45 seconds, Is Jack's statement correct? Provide evidence to support your answer. [5]

The distance is the area.

For the first 45 seconds,

$$S_1 = \frac{10 \times 10}{2} + \frac{10 + 50}{2} \times 10 + 25 \times 50 = 1600 \text{ m}$$

For the second 45 seconds,

$$S_2 = \frac{20 + 50}{2} \times 10 + 20 \times 10 + \frac{20 \times 25}{2} = 800 \text{ m}$$

So Jack is correct.

(c) After T seconds, the carriage has travelled 600 m. Find the value of T. [3]

For the first 20 seconds,

$$S_3 = \frac{10 \times 10}{2} + \frac{10 + 50}{2} \times 10 = 350 \text{ m}$$

$600 - 350 = 250$ m

After 20 seconds, the carriage moves further 250 m at the velocity 50 m s^{-1}.

$$t = \frac{250}{50} = 5 \text{ s}$$

Therefore $T = 20 + t = 20 + 5 = 25$ s

11 Masses A of 0.2 kg and B of 0.4 kg are attached to the ends of a light, inextensible string which hangs over a smooth pulley as shown in the diagram. Initially B is held at rest 2 m above the ground. A rests on the ground with the string taut. Then B is let go.

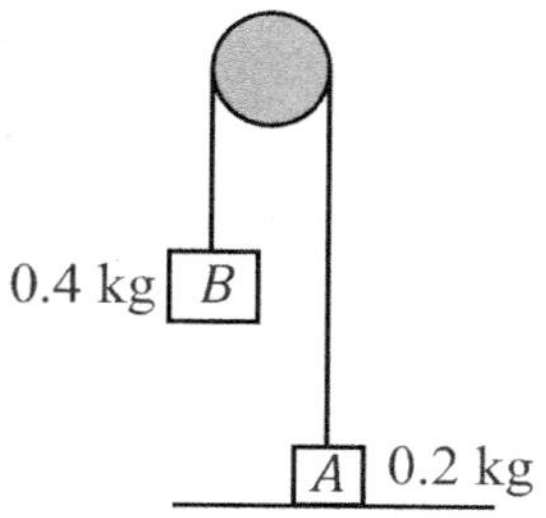

(a) Draw a diagram for each mass showing the forces acting on it and the direction of its acceleration at a later time when A and B are moving with an acceleration of a m s^{-2} and before B hits the ground. [3]

(b) Write down the equation of each mass in the direction it moves. [3]

$0.4g - T = 0.4a$ (1)

$T - 0.2g = 0.2a$ (2)

(c) Use your equation to find a and the tension in the string. Give your answers to 3 significant figures. [2]

Eqs. (1)+(2)

$$0.2g = 0.6a \Rightarrow a = \frac{0.2g}{0.6} = \frac{0.2 \times 9.8}{0.6} = 3.27 \text{ m s}^{-2}$$

$$T = 0.2a + 0.2g = 0.2 \times 3.27 + 0.2 \times 9.8 = 2.61 \text{ N}$$

(d) Find the time taken for B to hit the ground. Give your answers to 3 significant figures. [2]

$$s = \frac{1}{2} \times at^2 \Rightarrow t = \sqrt{\frac{2s}{a}} = \sqrt{\frac{2 \times 2}{3.27}} = 1.11 \text{ s}$$

(e) State any assumptions made in your model. [2]

There is no air resistance. The string does not break.

Paper 2 solutions

Section A: Pure Mathematics

1 Points S, T, U and V make a parallelogram, $STUV$. The position vectors of S, T and V are $\begin{bmatrix}1\\1\end{bmatrix}$, $\begin{bmatrix}8\\1\end{bmatrix}$ and $\begin{bmatrix}-2\\6\end{bmatrix}$ respectively. Find the distance between S and U. Give your answer in exact surd form. [4]

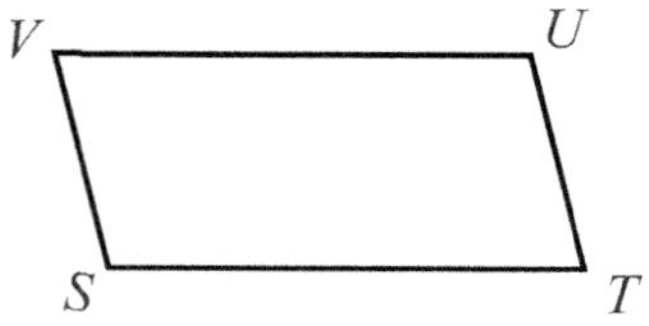

As points S, T, U and V make a parallelogram,

$\overrightarrow{VU} = \overrightarrow{ST}$

$\overrightarrow{SU} = \overrightarrow{SV} + \overrightarrow{VU} = \overrightarrow{SV} + \overrightarrow{ST} = \overrightarrow{OV} - \overrightarrow{OS} + \overrightarrow{OT} - \overrightarrow{OS} = \overrightarrow{OV} + \overrightarrow{OT} - 2\overrightarrow{OS}$

$= \begin{bmatrix}-2\\6\end{bmatrix} + \begin{bmatrix}8\\1\end{bmatrix} - 2\begin{bmatrix}1\\1\end{bmatrix} = \begin{bmatrix}4\\5\end{bmatrix}$

$\left|\overrightarrow{SU}\right| = \sqrt{4^2 + 5^2} = \sqrt{41}$

2 It is given that $(x-1)$ and $(x-2)$ are two factors of $f(x)$, where

$f(x) = x^3 - 2x^2 + px + q$

(a) Find the value of p and the value of q. [2]

$f(1) = 0 \Rightarrow 1^3 - 2 \times 1^2 + p \times 1 + q = 0 \Rightarrow p + q = 1$

$f(2) = 0 \Rightarrow 2^3 - 2 \times 2^2 + p \times 2 + q = 0 \Rightarrow 2p + q = 0$

$\Rightarrow p = -1,\ q = 2$

$f(x) = x^3 - 2x^2 - x + 2$

(b) Fully factorise $f(x)$. [2]

$(x-1)(x-2) = x^2 - 3x + 2$

$f(x) = x^3 - 2x^2 - x + 2 = (x^2 - 3x + 2)(x+1) = (x-1)(x-2)(x+1)$

3 The diagram shows triangle OAB, with $OA = 4$ cm, $OB = 6$ cm and $AB = 2\sqrt{7}$ cm.

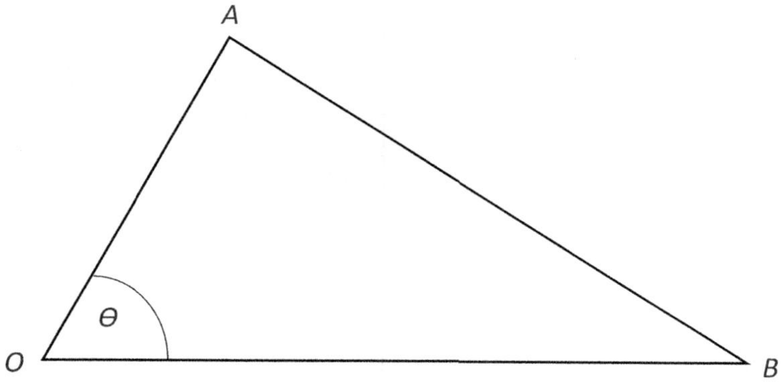

(a) Find the exact size of angle AOB. [2]

$AB^2 = OA^2 + OB^2 - 2 \times OA \times OB \times \cos\theta$

$\Rightarrow \cos\theta = \dfrac{OA^2 + OB^2 - AB^2}{2 \times OA \times OB} = \dfrac{16 + 36 - 28}{2 \times 4 \times 6} = \dfrac{1}{2}$

Angle AOB is $\dfrac{\pi}{3}$ or $60°$

(b) Find the area of triangle OAB. [2]

The area of triangle OAB is

$$\frac{OA \times OB \times \sin\theta}{2} = \frac{4 \times 6 \times \frac{\sqrt{3}}{2}}{2} = 6\sqrt{3}\ \text{cm}^2$$

4 Point C has coordinates $(c, 2)$ and point D has coordinates $(6, d)$. The line $y + 4x = 11$ is the perpendicular bisector of CD.

Find c and d. [4]

The middle point CD is M.

$M_x = \dfrac{c+6}{2}, M_y = \dfrac{2+d}{2}$

Point M lies on the line $y + 4x = 11$

$\dfrac{2+d}{2} + 4 \times \dfrac{c+6}{2} = 11 \Rightarrow 4c + d = -4$ (1)

The line $y + 4x = 11$ is the perpendicular bisector of CD

The gradient of CD is

$\dfrac{1}{4}$

$\dfrac{2-d}{c-6} = \dfrac{1}{4} \Rightarrow c + 4d = 14$ (2)

Solve Eqs. (1) and (2), we have

$c = -2, d = 4$

5 The graph of the equation $y = \dfrac{2}{x}$ is translated by the vector $\begin{bmatrix} 3 \\ 2 \end{bmatrix}$

(a) Write down the equation of the transformed graph. [2]

$y = \dfrac{2}{x-3} + 2$

(b) State the equation of the asymptotes of the transformed graph. [4]

Vertical asymptote:

$x \longrightarrow 3^- \Rightarrow y \rightarrow -\infty$

$x \longrightarrow 3^+ \Rightarrow y \rightarrow +\infty$

Vertical asymptote is $x = 3$

Horizontal asymptote:

$x \longrightarrow \infty \Rightarrow y \rightarrow 2$

Horizontal asymptote is $y = 2$

Asymptotes are $x = 3; y = 2$.

6 (a) Sketch the curve $y = (x - a)^2(3 - x)$, where $0 < a < 3$, indicating the coordinates of the points where the curve and the axes meet. [6]

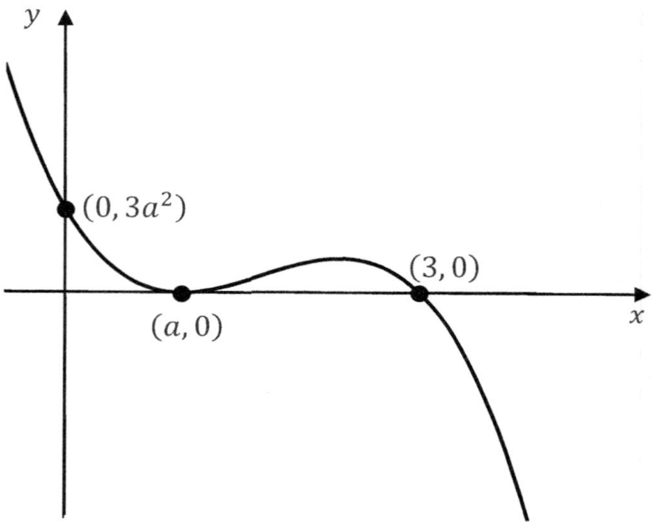

(b) Hence, solve $(x - a)^2(3 - x) > 0$, giving your answer in set notation form. [2]

$\{x: x < a\} \cup \{x: a < x < 3\}$

7 The number of employees, p, working for a company t years after it was founded can be modelled by the equation $p = at^b$. The table below shows the number of employees the company has:

Age of company (t years)	3	6	9	12	15
Number of employees (p)	4	8	10	14	16

(a) Show that $p = at^b$ can be written in the form $\log_{10} p = b\log_{10} t + \log_{10} a$.

[4]

$p = at^b$

Take logs of both sides.

$\log_{10} p = \log_{10}(at^b) \Rightarrow \log_{10} p = \log_{10}(t^b) + \log_{10} a \Rightarrow$

$\log_{10} p = b\log_{10} t + \log_{10} a$

Therefore $\log_{10} p = b\log_{10} t + \log_{10} a$

(b) Plot a graph of $\log_{10} p$ against $\log_{10} t$ and draw a line of best fit for your graph.

[4]

$\log_{10} t$	0.477	0.778	0.954	1.079	1.176
$\log_{10} p$	0.602	0.903	1.000	1.146	1.204

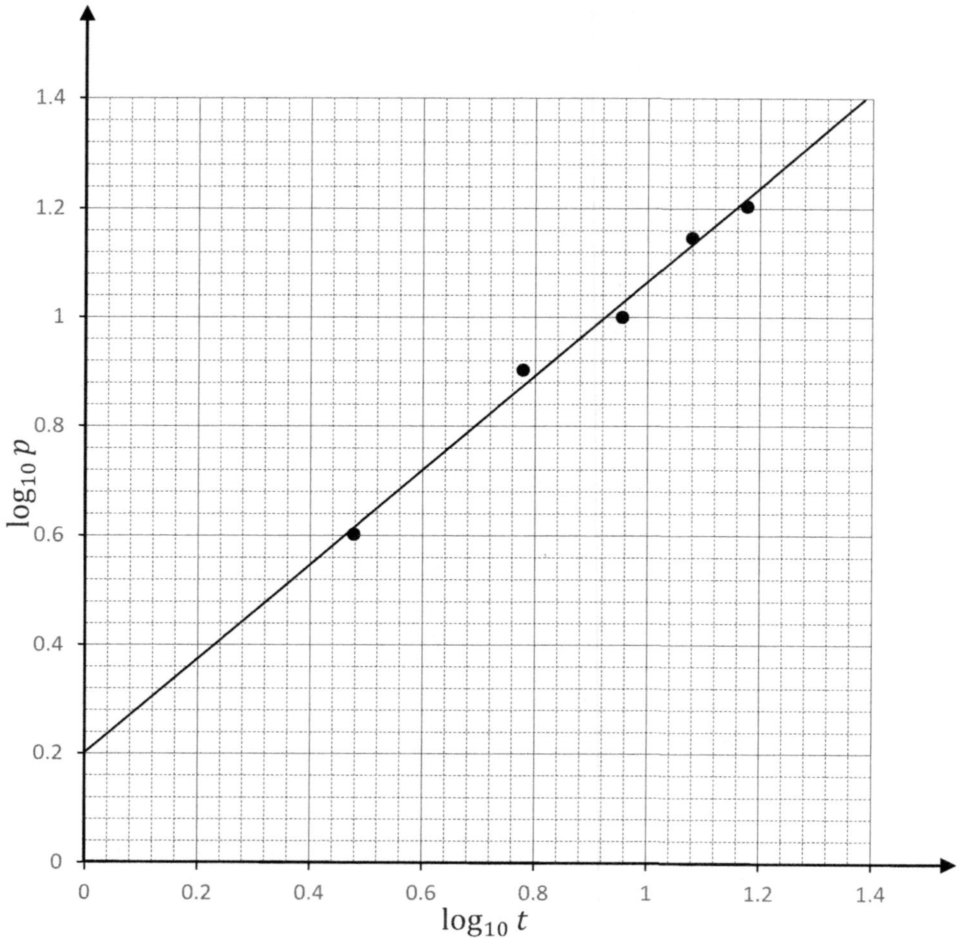

(c) Use your graph to estimate the values of a and b in the equation $p = at^b$.

Give your answer to 3 decimal places. [4]

From part (a), the graph has equation $\log_{10} p = b \log_{10} t + \log_{10} a$

Compare this to line equation $y = mx + c$

b is the gradient to the line and $\log_{10} a$ is the vertical-axis intercept of the line.

Use the coordinates of two points (0, 0.2) and (0.6, 0.72) on the line to find the gradient and the vertical intercept of the line.

$$b = \frac{0.72 - 0.2}{0.6 - 0} = 0.867$$

$$\log_{10} a = 0.2 \Rightarrow a = 10^{0.2} = 1.585$$

$$p = 1.585t^{0.867}.$$

8 A quadratic function $f(x)$ is defined on $\mathbb{R}$. The turning point is (2, 2).

$h(x) = af(x + b) + c$, and the turning point is (7, -8). The diagram shows the graphs with equations $y = f(x)$ and $y = h(x)$.

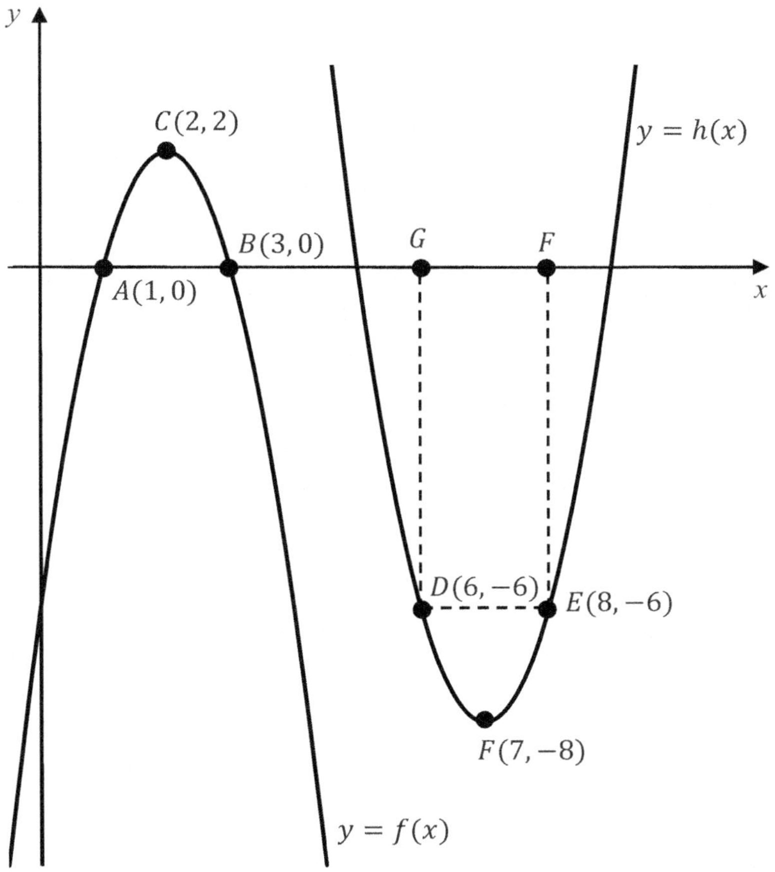

(a) Find the values of a, b and c. [4]

From the graphs of $y = f(x)$ and $y = h(x)$, the graph of $y = h(x)$ can be obtained by the following steps:

Step 1: the graph of $y = f(x)$ is translated horizontally right 5 units to obtain $y = f(x + b)$.

Step 2: the graph of $y = f(x + b)$ is reflected over the x-axis to obtain $y = -f(x + b)$.

Step 3: the graph of $y = -f(x + b)$ is translated vertically down 6 units to obtain $y = -f(x + b) - 6$, which is $y = h(x)$.

Therefore $a = -1, b = -5, c = -6$.

(b) It is known that $\int_1^3 f(x)\mathrm{d}x = \frac{8}{3}$. Find the value of $\int_6^8 h(x)\mathrm{d}x$. [4]

The area of rectangle *DEFG* is $2 \times 6 = 12$

$$\int_6^8 h(x)\mathrm{d}x = -\int_1^3 f(x)\mathrm{d}x - 12 = -\frac{8}{3} - 12 = -\frac{44}{3}$$

Section B: Mechanics

9 (a) The movement of a particle is modelled by vector **p**. The particle is travelling at a speed of 6 m s^{-1} with direction of 30° above the horizontal. Write the vector **p** in the form of $a\mathbf{i} + b\mathbf{j}$, where $a, b \in \mathbb{R}$. [2]

$\mathbf{p} = 6\cos 30°\,\mathbf{i} + 6\sin 30°\,\mathbf{j} = 3\sqrt{3}\mathbf{i} + 3\mathbf{j}$

(b) The particle strikes another particle. Its movement is now modelled by vector $\mathbf{q} = 2\sqrt{2}(\mathbf{i} + \mathbf{j})$.

Find the amount by which the particle's speed has decreased, and state the particle's new direction. [3]

$|\mathbf{q}| = \sqrt{(2\sqrt{2})^2 + (2\sqrt{2})^2} = 4$ m s^{-1}

So the particle's speed has decreased 2 m s^{-1}.

$\tan\theta = \frac{1}{1} = 1 \Rightarrow \theta = 45°$

The particle's new direction is 45° above the horizontal.

10 An ice skater of mass 55 kg is initially moving with speed 2 m s^{-1} and glides to a halt over a distance of 10 m. Assuming that the force of resistance is constant, find

(a) the value of the resistance force [3]

$v^2 = u^2 + 2as \Rightarrow a = \frac{v^2 - u^2}{2s} = \frac{0 - 2^2}{2 \times 10} = -0.2 \text{ m s}^{-2}$

$P - F = ma \Rightarrow F = P - ma = 0 - 55 \times (-0.2) = 11 \text{ N}$

(b) the distance he would travel gliding to rest from an initial speed of 8 m s^{-1}. [2]

$v^2 = u^2 + 2as \Rightarrow s = \frac{v^2 - u^2}{2a} = \frac{0 - 8^2}{2 \times (-0.2)} = 160 \text{ m}$

(c) the force he would need to apply to maintain a steady speed of 10 m s^{-1}. [2]

The forces on ice skater must be in equilibrium, because he is moving at a constant speed, so he would need to apply 11 N to maintain a steady speed.

11 The diagram shows a block of mass 5 kg lying on a smooth table. It is attached to a block of mass 3 kg by a string which passes over a smooth pulley. The tension in the string is T, as shown, and the block has acceleration a m s^{-2}.

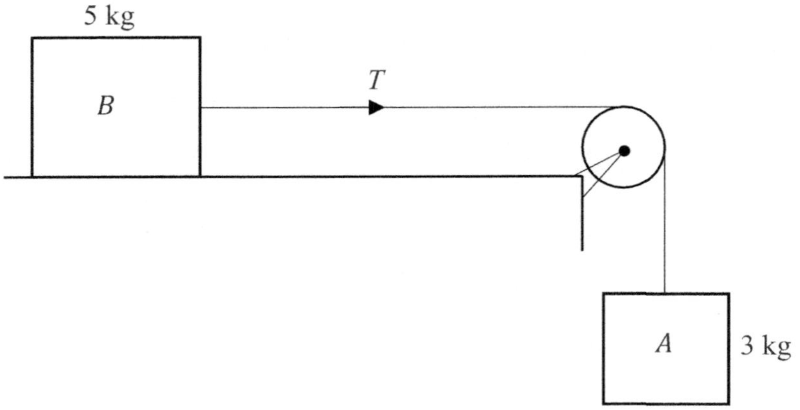

(a) Draw a diagram for each block, showing all the forces acting on it. [4]

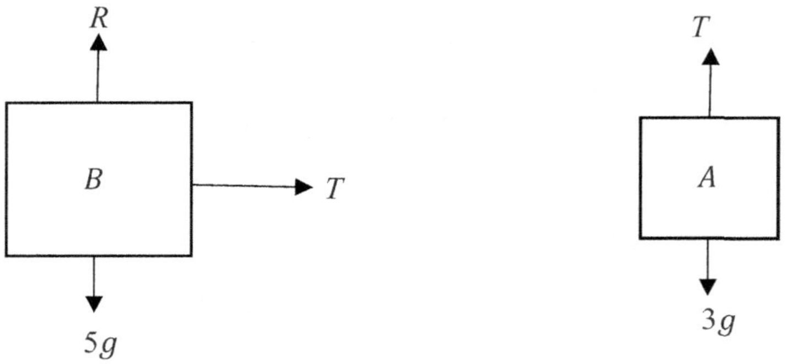

(b) Write down the equation of motion for each of the blocks. [2]

$T = 5a$ (1) $3g - T = 3a$ (2)

(c) Use your equation to find the values of a and T. Give your answers to 3 significant figures. [4]

Eqs. (1)+(2)⇒

$$3g = 8a \Rightarrow a = \frac{3g}{8} = \frac{3 \times 9.8}{8} = 3.68 \text{ m s}^{-2}$$

$$T = 5a = 5 \times 3.68 = 18.4 \text{ N}$$

(d) In practice, the table is not truly smooth and a is found to be 2.5 m s^{-2}. Use your new equations to find the frictional force that would produce this result.

[3]

$T - F = 5a$ (3) $3g - T = 3a$ (4)

Eqs. (3)+(4)$\Rightarrow 3g - F = 8a \Rightarrow F = 3g - 8a = 3 \times 9.8 - 8 \times 2.5 = 9.4$ N

Paper 3 solutions

Section A: Pure Mathematics

1 The coefficient of x^2 in the binomial expansion of $(1+3x)^n$ where $n > 0$ is 495.

Find the value of n. [3]

$${}^nC_2(3x)^2 = 495x^2 \Rightarrow \frac{n!}{2!\,(n-2)!} \times 9 = 495 \Rightarrow \frac{n(n-1)}{2} \times 9 = 495 \Rightarrow$$

$n(n-1) = 110 \Rightarrow (n-11)(n+10) = 0 \Rightarrow n = 11, \text{as } n > 0$

So the value of n is 11.

2 *ABCD* is a kite where *A* is the point (1, -2), *B* is the point (7, 1) and *C* is the point (3, 4). *AC* perpendicularly bisects *BD*.

(a) Find the equation of the line *AC* in the form $y = mx + c$. [2]

The gradient of line *AC* can be calculated as follows.

$$\frac{4+2}{3-1} = 3$$

The equation of line *AC* can be obtained as follows.

$y + 2 = 3(x-1) \Rightarrow y = 3x - 5$ (1)

(b) Find the coordinates of point *D*. [4]

The gradient of line *BD* is

$$-\frac{1}{3}$$

The line *BD* can be obtained as follows.

$$y - 1 = -\frac{1}{3}(x-7) \Rightarrow 3y + x = 10$$

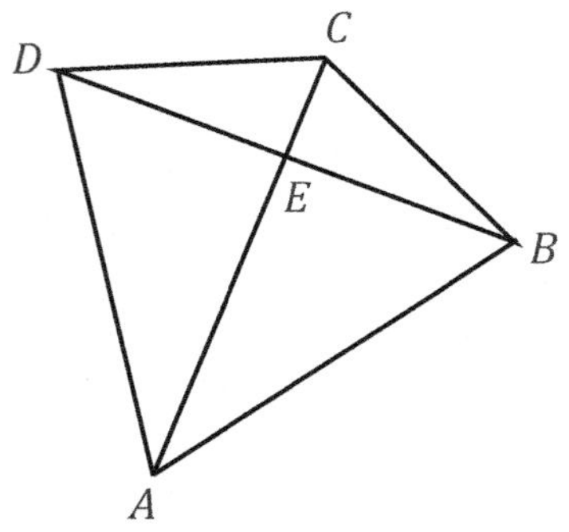

Substitute Eq. (1) into the above equation.

$$3(3x-5) + x = 10 \Rightarrow x = \frac{5}{2}$$

$$y = 3x - 5 = 3 \times \frac{5}{2} - 5 = \frac{5}{2}$$

Lines *BD* and *AC* intersect at *E*

$$\left(\frac{5}{2}, \frac{5}{2}\right)$$

Point *E* is the midpoint of *BD*

$$x_D = 2x_E - x_B = 2 \times \frac{5}{2} - 7 = -2$$

$$y_D = 2y_E - y_B = 2 \times \frac{5}{2} - 1 = 4$$

The coordinates of point *D* are (-2, 4).

(c) Find the area of the kite. [2]

The area of the kite can be calculated as follows.

$$\frac{AC \times BD}{2} = \frac{\sqrt{(3-1)^2 + (4+2)^2} \times \sqrt{(-2-7)^2 + (4-1)^2}}{2} = 30 \text{ square units}$$

3 (a) Show that the equation $9\cos\theta + \sin\theta\tan\theta - 6 = 0$ can be expressed as the equation $(2\cos\theta - 1)(4\cos\theta - 1) = 0$ [2]

$9\cos\theta + \sin\theta\tan\theta - 6 = 0 \Rightarrow 9\cos^2\theta + \sin^2\theta - 6\cos\theta = 0 \Rightarrow$

$8\cos^2\theta + \cos^2\theta + \sin^2\theta - 6\cos\theta = 0 \Rightarrow 8\cos^2\theta + 1 - 6\cos\theta = 0 \Rightarrow$

$(2\cos\theta - 1)(4\cos\theta - 1) = 0$

Therefore the equation $9\cos\theta + \sin\theta\tan\theta - 6 = 0$ can be expressed as the equation $(2\cos\theta - 1)(4\cos\theta - 1) = 0$

(b) Find all the values of θ that solve the equation

$9\cos\theta + \sin\theta\tan\theta - 6 = 0$

for $-180° \le \theta \le 180°$

Give your answer to the nearest degree. [2]

$2\cos\theta - 1 = 0 \Rightarrow \theta = \pm 60°$

$4\cos\theta - 1 = 0 \Rightarrow \theta = \pm 76°$

All the values of θ are $\pm 60°$ and $\pm 76°$

(c) Hence, find all the solutions of the equation

$9\cos\frac{\theta}{2} + \sin\frac{\theta}{2}\tan\frac{\theta}{2} - 6 = 0$

for $-180° \le \theta \le 180°$

Give your answer to the nearest degree. [2]

$2\cos\frac{\theta}{2} - 1 = 0 \Rightarrow \theta = \pm 120°$

$4\cos\frac{\theta}{2} - 1 = 0 \Rightarrow \theta = \pm 151°$

All the values of θ are $\pm 120°$ and $\pm 151°$

4 In this question you must show detailed reasoning.

A curve has equation

$$y = \frac{a}{\sqrt{x}} + bx^2 + \frac{c}{x^3}$$

where $x > 0$, a, b and c are positive constants.

The curve has a single turning point.

Use the second derivative of y to determine the nature of this turning point.

You do not need to find the coordinates of the turning point. [6]

$$\frac{\mathrm{d}y}{\mathrm{d}x} = -\frac{1}{2}ax^{-\frac{3}{2}} + 2bx - 3cx^{-4}$$

$$\frac{\mathrm{d}^2y}{\mathrm{d}x^2} = -\frac{1}{2} \times \left(-\frac{3}{2}\right) ax^{-\frac{5}{2}} + 2b + 12cx^{-5} = \frac{3}{4}ax^{-\frac{5}{2}} + 2b + 12cx^{-5}$$

As $x > 0$, a, b and c are positive constants, all the terms in the second derivative of y are positive, therefore

$$\frac{\mathrm{d}^2y}{\mathrm{d}x^2} > 0$$

The turning point is a minimum.

5 Curve C has equation $y = x^2$, C is translated by vector $\begin{bmatrix}3\\0\end{bmatrix}$ to give curve C_1.

Line L has equation $y = x$, L is stretched by scale factor 2 parallel to the x-axis to give line L_1.

Find the exact distance between the two intersection points of C_1 and L_1 [5]

Curve C_1: $y = (x-3)^2$ (1)

Line L_1: $y = \frac{x}{2}$ (2)

Eqs $(1) - (2) \Rightarrow (x-3)^2 = \frac{x}{2} \Rightarrow (x-2)(2x-9) = 0 \Rightarrow x = 2, \frac{9}{2}$

$x = 2 \Rightarrow y = 1; x = \frac{9}{2} \Rightarrow y = \frac{9}{4}$

The intersection points are:

$(2, 1)$and $(\frac{9}{2}, \frac{9}{4})$

The distance between the two intersection points is:

$$\sqrt{(2 - \frac{9}{2})^2 + (1 - \frac{9}{4})^2} = \frac{5\sqrt{5}}{4}$$

6 A circle has equation $x^2 + y^2 + 10x - 4y - 71 = 0$

(a) Find the centre of the circle. [2]

$x^2 + y^2 + 10x - 4y - 71 = 0 \Rightarrow (x+5)^2 + (y-2)^2 = 42$

The centre is (-5, 2).

(b) Hence, find the equation of the tangent to the circle at the point (1, 10), giving your answer in the form $ax + bx + c = 0$, where a, b and c are integers. [3]

The gradient of the line passing through the centre of the circle and the point (1, 10) is

$\frac{10-2}{1+5} = \frac{4}{3} \Rightarrow$ the gradient of the tangent is $-\frac{3}{4}$

The equation of the tangent can be given by

$$y - 10 = -\frac{3}{4}(x-1) \Rightarrow 3x + 4y - 43 = 0$$

7 (a) Find

$$\int (4x - x^3)\mathrm{d}x$$ [2]

$$\int (4x - x^3)\mathrm{d}x = 2x^2 - \frac{x^4}{4} + c$$

(b) Evaluate

$$\int_{-2}^{2} (4x - x^3)\mathrm{d}x$$ [2]

$$\int_{-2}^{2} (4x - x^3)\mathrm{d}x = \left[2x^2 - \frac{x^4}{4}\right]_{-2}^{2} = 0$$

(c) Using a sketch, explain why the integral in part (b) does not give the area enclosed between the curve $y = 4x - x^3$ and the x-axis. [3]

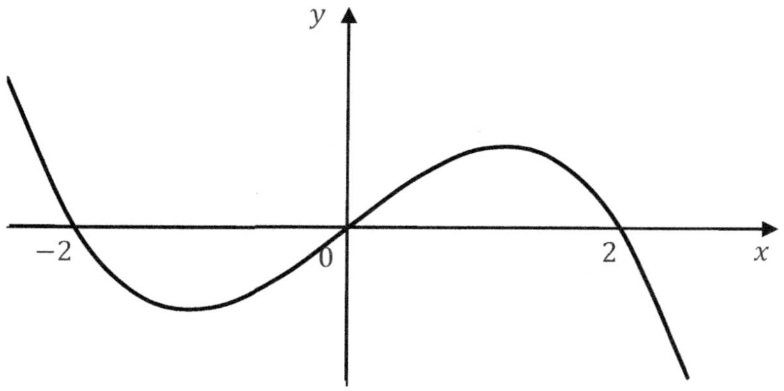

The area between -2 and 0 is equal to the area between 0 and 2. However the area between -2 and 0 lies below the axis so its integral has a negative value, the area between 0 and 2 lies above the axis so its integral has a positive value. Therefore its integral between -2 and 2 is zero.

(d) Find the area enclosed between the curve $y = 4x - x^3$ and the x-axis. [2]

Area is:

$$2\int_0^2 (4x - x^3)\mathrm{d}x = 2\left[2x^2 - \frac{x^4}{4}\right]_0^2 = 2 \times (8 - 4) = 8$$

8 The yearly income from book sales of a particular author has tended to increase with time. The table below shows his income from book sales over the first five years after his book was published.

Number of years after book published (t)	1	2	3	4	5
Income (£p thousand)	10	13	17	24	35

The relationship is modelled by the equation $p = ab^t$, where a and b are constants to be found.

(a) Plot a graph of $\log_{10} p$ against t and draw a line of best fit for your graph. [3]

t	1	2	3	4	5
$\log_{10} p$	1	1.114	1.230	1.380	1.554

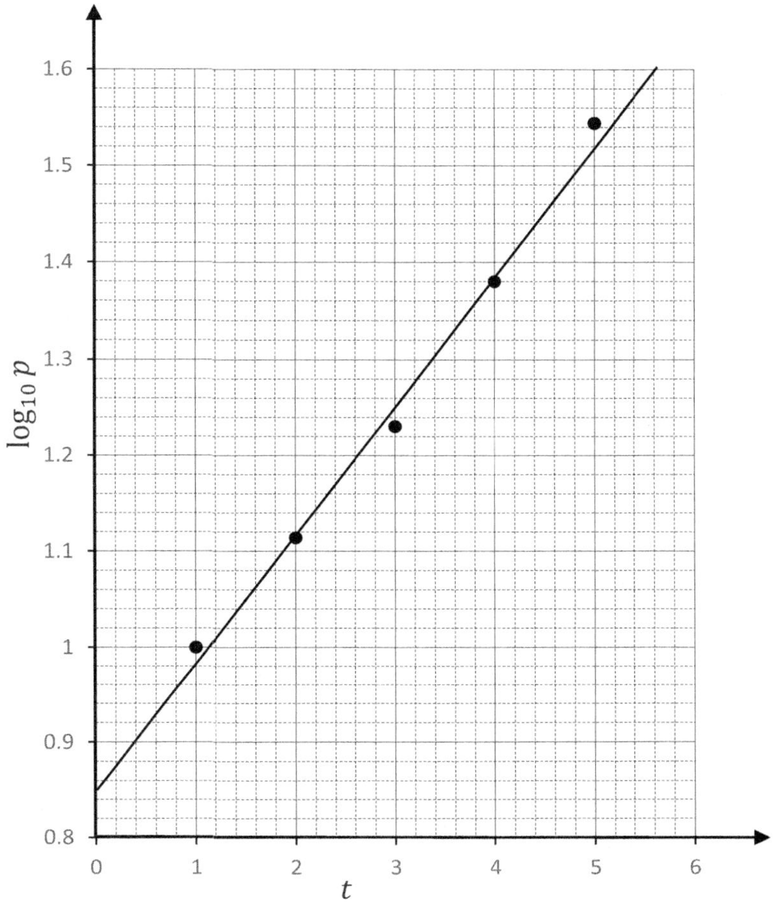

(b) State, in terms of a and b, the gradient and vertical-axis intercept of your graph.

Hence use your graph to find the values of a and b. Give your answers to 3 significant figures. [3]

$p = ab^t$

Take logs of both sides.

$\log_{10} p = \log_{10}(ab^t) \Rightarrow \log_{10} p = t\log_{10}(b) + \log_{10} a$

Compare this to line equation $y = mx + c$

$\log_{10}(b)$ is the gradient to the line and $\log_{10} a$ is the vertical-axis intercept of the line.

Use the coordinates of two points (0, 0.85) and (2, 1.12) on the line to find the gradient and the vertical intercept of the line.

$$\log_{10}(b) = \frac{1.12 - 0.85}{2 - 0} = 0.14 \Rightarrow b = 10^{0.14} = 1.38$$

$\log_{10} a = 0.85 \Rightarrow a = 10^{0.85} = 7.08$

$p = 7.08 \times 1.38^t$.

(c) Predict the author's income 10 years after his book was published. [1]

$p = 7.08 \times 1.38^{10} = 177.35$.

The author's income will be approximately £177350.

(d) Suggest one reason why the prediction in part (c) might not be accurate. [1]

10 years is large extrapolation from the data.

Section B: Mechanics

9 Two forces, $(x\mathbf{i} + y\mathbf{j})$N and $(5\mathbf{i} + \mathbf{j})$N, act on a particle P of mass 2.5 kg. The resultant of the two forces is $(8\mathbf{i} - 3\mathbf{j})$N. Find

(a) the values of x and y. [2]

$(8\mathbf{i} - 3\mathbf{j}) = (x\mathbf{i} + y\mathbf{j}) + (5\mathbf{i} + \mathbf{j}) \Rightarrow x = 8 - 5 = 3, y = -3 - 1 = -4$

(b) the magnitude and direction of the acceleration of P, giving your answers to 3 significant figures. [3]

$$\mathbf{a} = \frac{\mathbf{F}}{m} = \frac{8\mathbf{i} - 3\mathbf{j}}{2.5} = \frac{8\mathbf{i} - 3\mathbf{j}}{2.5} = 3.2\mathbf{i} - 1.2\mathbf{j}$$

$$|\mathbf{a}| = \sqrt{3.2^2 + (-1.2)^2} = 3.42 \text{ m s}^{-2}$$

$$\tan\theta = \frac{-1.2}{3.2} \Rightarrow \theta \approx 339°$$

(c) the particle's velocity vector, 5 seconds after it accelerates from rest. [2]

$\mathbf{v} = \mathbf{u} + \mathbf{a}t = (0\mathbf{i} + 0\mathbf{j}) + (3.2\mathbf{i} - 1.2\mathbf{j}) \times 5 = (16\mathbf{i} - 6\mathbf{j}) \text{ m s}^{-1}$

10 A particle sets off from the origin O at $t = 0$ s and moves in a straight line. At time t seconds, the velocity of the particle is v m s^{-1}, where

$$v = \begin{cases} 9t - 3t^2 & 0 \leq t \leq 2\text{ s} \\ \dfrac{24}{t^2} & t > 2\text{ s} \end{cases}$$

(a) Sketch the graph of the velocity of the particle against time. [3]

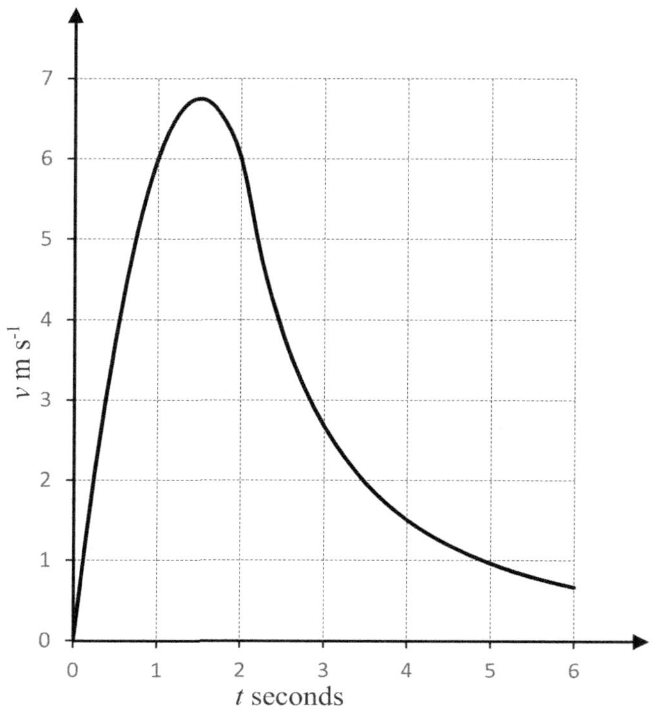

(b) Find the maximum speed of the particle in the interval $0 \leq t \leq 2$ s [3]

v is at a maximum when

$$\frac{dv}{dt} = 0$$

$$\frac{dv}{dt} = 9 - 6t = 0 \Rightarrow t = 1.5 \Rightarrow v = 9 \times 1.5 - 3 \times 1.5^2 = 6.75\text{ m s}^{-1}$$

(c) Find the displacement of the particle from O at

(i) $t = 2$ s [2]

$$s = \int_0^2 (9t - 3t^2)dt = \left[\frac{9t^2}{2} - t^3\right]_0^2 = \frac{9 \times 2^2}{2} - 2^3 = 10\text{ m}$$

(ii) $t = 6$ s [2]

$$s = \int_0^2 (9t - 3t^2)\text{d}t + \int_2^6 \frac{24}{t^2}\text{d}t = 10 - \left[\frac{24}{t}\right]_2^6 = 10 - (4 - 12) = 18 \text{ m}$$

11 The diagram shows two particles, A and B. A is of mass $3m$ kg and rests on a rough plane with coefficient of friction 0.25. A is connected to B by a light inextensible string which passes over a smooth pulley. B is of mass $2m$ kg and hangs freely. The system is released from rest with the string taut.

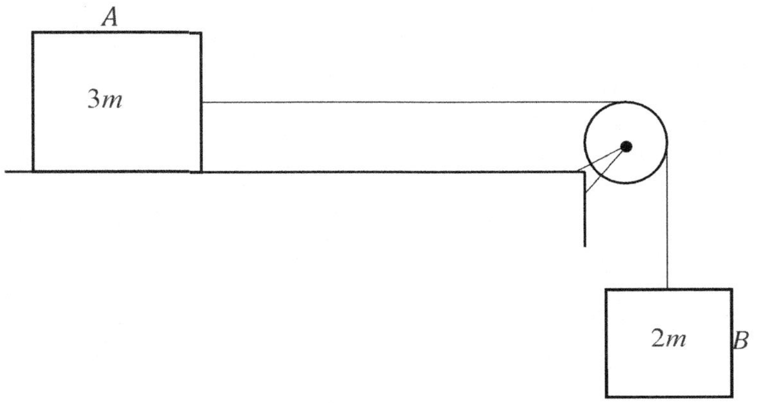

(a) Find the initial acceleration of the system in terms of g. [2]

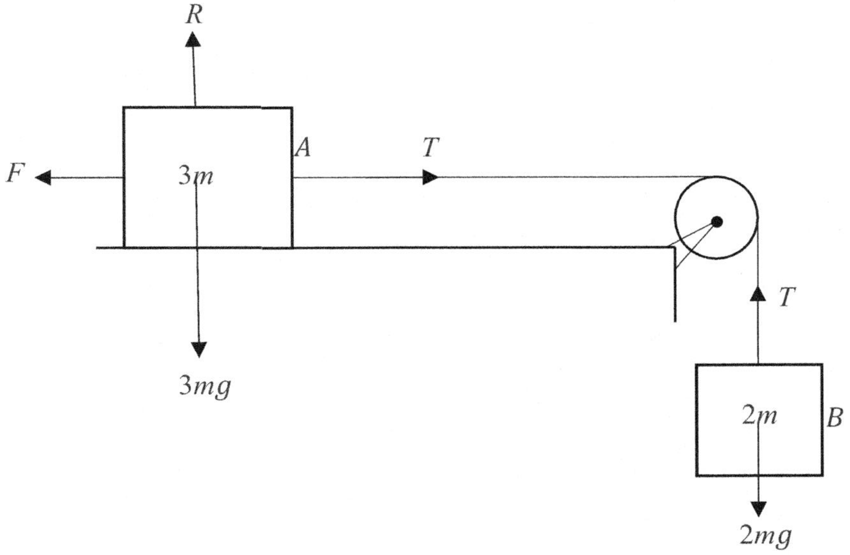

For particle B: $2mg - T = 2ma$ (1)

For particle A: $T - 3mg\mu = 3ma$ (2)

Eqs. (1)+((2)⇒ $2mg - 3mg\mu = 5ma \Rightarrow$

$$a = \frac{2g - 3g\mu}{5} = \frac{2g - 3g \times 0.25}{5} = 0.25g$$

(b) The system is release with B 1 m above the ground. When B hits the ground, the string goes slack. Find the total distance moved by A before coming to rest again, assuming that it does not hit the pulley. [4]

When B hits the ground, the speed is v m s^{-1}.

$$v^2 = u^2 + 2as \Rightarrow v = \sqrt{u^2 + 2as} = \sqrt{0^2 + 2 \times 0.25g \times 1} = \sqrt{0.5g}$$

A will deaccelerate due to the fraction. Let a_A be the acceleration of A, s_A the distance moved by A after B hits the ground.

$$u_A = \sqrt{0.5g}, v_A = 0$$

$$T - 3mg\mu = 3ma_A, T = 0 \Rightarrow a_A = -g\mu = -0.25g$$

$$v_A^2 = u_A^2 + 2a_A s_A \Rightarrow s_A = \frac{v_A^2 - u_A^2}{2a_A} = \frac{-0.5g}{2 \times (-0.25g)} = 1 \text{ m}$$

The total distance moved by A before coming to rest again is

$1 + 1 = 2$ m.

(c) State where you have used the assumption that the pulley is smooth. [2]

By making the tensions at each end of the string equal.

Paper 4 solutions

Section A: Pure Mathematics

1 It is given that $\cos 15° = \dfrac{\sqrt{3}+1}{2\sqrt{2}}, \sin 15° = \dfrac{\sqrt{3}-1}{2\sqrt{2}}$

Find the exact value of tan 15°, giving your answer in the form $a - \sqrt{b}\,, a, b \in \mathbb{Z}^+$.

[3]

$$\tan 15° = \frac{\sqrt{3}-1}{\sqrt{3}+1} = \frac{(\sqrt{3}-1)(\sqrt{3}-1)}{(\sqrt{3}+1)(\sqrt{3}-1)} = \frac{4-2\sqrt{3}}{2} = 2-\sqrt{3}$$

2 (a) Using $y = 2^{2x}$ as a substitution, show that

$16^x - 2^{(2x+3)} - 9 = 0$ can be written as $y^2 - 8y - 9 = 0$ [2]

$$16^x - 2^{(2x+3)} - 9 = 0 \Rightarrow 2^{4x} - 8 \times 2^{2x} - 9 = 0 \xRightarrow{y=2^{2x}} y^2 - 8y - 9 = 0$$

(b) Hence, solve the equation $16^x - 2^{(2x+3)} - 9 = 0$, giving the exact value of x.

[3]

$y^2 - 8y - 9 = 0 \Rightarrow (y-9)(y+1) = 0 \Rightarrow y = 9, -1$

As $y = 2^{2x} > 0$, $y = 9$ is its only solution here.

$2^{2x} = 9 \Rightarrow 2x = \log_2 9 \Rightarrow 2x = 2\log_2 3 \Rightarrow x = \log_2 3$

3 (a) Express $2x^2 - 8x + k$ in the form $a(x-b)^2 + c$ [2]

$2x^2 - 8x + k = 2(x-2)^2 - 8 + k$

(b) Find the value of k for which the curve $y = 2x^2 - 8x + k$ does not intersect the line $y = 4$ [3]

$y = 2x^2 - 8x + k = 2(x-2)^2 - 8 + k$

It has a minimum point at $(2, -8+k)$

If $-8 + k > 4 \Rightarrow k > 12$, it does not intersect the line $y = 4$.

4 (a) Show that $\sin\theta = 1$ is one solution of the equation

$5\cos^2\theta + 6\sin\theta = 6$ [2]

$5(1-\sin^2\theta) + 6\sin\theta = 6 \Rightarrow 5\sin^2\theta - 6\sin\theta + 1 = 0 \Rightarrow$

$(\sin\theta - 1)(5\sin\theta - 1) = 0 \Rightarrow \sin\theta = 1$ or $5\sin\theta = 1$

Therefore $\sin\theta = 1$ is one solution of the equation.

(b) Find all the values of θ that solve the equation

$5\cos^2\theta + 6\sin\theta = 6$

for $0° \leq \theta \leq 360°$

Give your answer to the nearest degree. [3]

$\sin\theta = 1 \Rightarrow \theta = 90°$

$5\sin\theta = 1 \Rightarrow \theta = 12°, 168°$

All the values of θ are $12°, 90°$ and $168°$

(c) Hence, find all the solutions of the equation

$5\cos^2 2\theta + 6\sin 2\theta = 6$

for $0° \leq \theta \leq 360°$

Give your answer to the nearest degree. [3]

$\sin 2\theta = 1 \Rightarrow \theta = 45°, 225°$

$5\sin 2\theta = 1 \Rightarrow \theta = 6°, 84°, 186°, 264°$

All the values of θ are $6°, 45°, 84°, 186°, 225°$ and $264°$

5 For each of the following statements, decide whether it is true or false. If true, give a proof; if false, give a counterexample.

(a) If n is any positive integer, then $2^n - 1$ is prime. [2]

For example, $n = 4, 2^4 - 1 = 15 = 3 \times 5$, which is not prime. So the statement is false.

(b) If the sum of the digits of a four-digit number is divisible by 3, then the four-digit number is also divisible by 3. [5]

Let n be a four-digit number such that

$n = a_3a_2a_1a_0$

We have that

$a_3 = p \times 10^3, a_2 = q \times 10^2, a_1 = r \times 10^1, a_0 = s \times 10^0,$

where $0 \leq q, r, s \leq 9$ and $0 < p \leq 9$.

$p + q + r + s = 3k, k \in \mathbb{Z}.$

$\Rightarrow n = p \times 10^3 + q \times 10^2 + r \times 10^1 + s \times 10^0, s = 3k - p - q - r$

$\Rightarrow n = p \times 10^3 + q \times 10^2 + r \times 10^1 + 3k - p - q - r$

$= p(10^3 - 1) + q(10^2 - 1) + r(10 - 1) + 3k$

$= 999p + 99q + 9r + 3k = 3(333p + 33q + 3r + k)$

Since $(333p + 33q + 3r + k) \in \mathbb{Z}$, it follows that n is divisible by 3. So the statement is true.

6 The diagram shows a sector AOB of a circle with centre O and radius r cm.

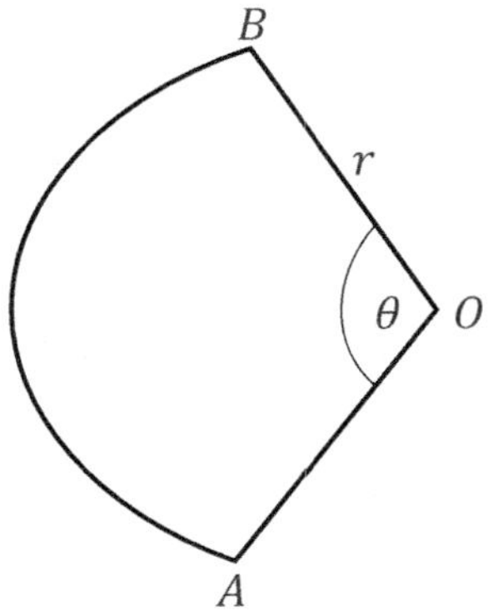

The angle AOB is θ radians. The sector has perimeter 30 cm.

(a) Find the area of the sector in terms of r. [3]

Perimeter of sector gives

$$30 = 2r + \theta r \Rightarrow \theta = \frac{30 - 2r}{r}$$

Area of sector can be calculated as follows.

$$S = \frac{1}{2}\theta r^2 = \frac{1}{2} \times \frac{30 - 2r}{r} \times r^2 = 15r - r^2$$

(b) Use calculus to find the value of r which maximises the area, and calculate the area and the angle AOB. [4]

$$\frac{\mathrm{d}S}{\mathrm{d}r} = 15 - 2r = 0 \Rightarrow r = 7.5 \text{ cm}$$

$$\frac{\mathrm{d}^2S}{\mathrm{d}r^2} = -2 < 0$$

$r = 7.5$ cm gives a maximum value for S, the area of sector.

$S = 15r - r^2 = 15 \times 7.5 - 7.5^2 = 56.25 \text{ cm}^2$

$$\theta = \frac{30 - 2r}{r} = \frac{30 - 2 \times 7.5}{7.5} = 2, \text{angle } AOB = 2 \text{ radians}$$

7 The diagram shows the graphs with equations $y = f(x)$ and $y = bf(x) + a$.

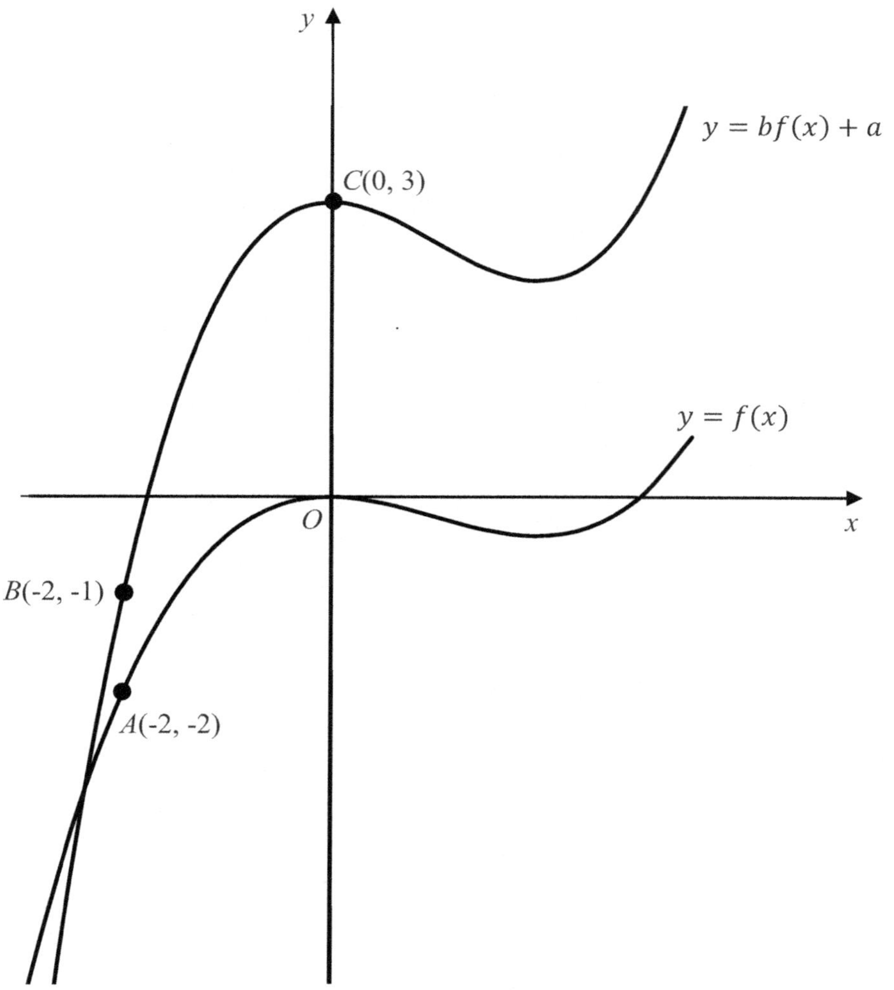

(a) Find the value of a. [4]

At the point O(0, 0), $f(0) = 0$; at the point C(0, 3), $3 = bf(0) + a \Rightarrow$

$3 = b \times 0 + a \Rightarrow a = 3$

(b) Find the value of b. [4]

At the point A(-2, -2), $f(-2) = -2$;

At the point B(-2, -1),), $-1 = bf(-2) + a \Rightarrow -1 = b \times (-2) + 3 \Rightarrow b = 2$

8 Susan is baking a birthday cake. She places the cake mix in a preheated oven. The temperature in the centre of the cake mix in °C is modelled by the function $H(t) = 180 - a(1.08)^{-t}$ where the time t is in minutes after the mix is placed in the oven, The graph of $H(t)$ is given.

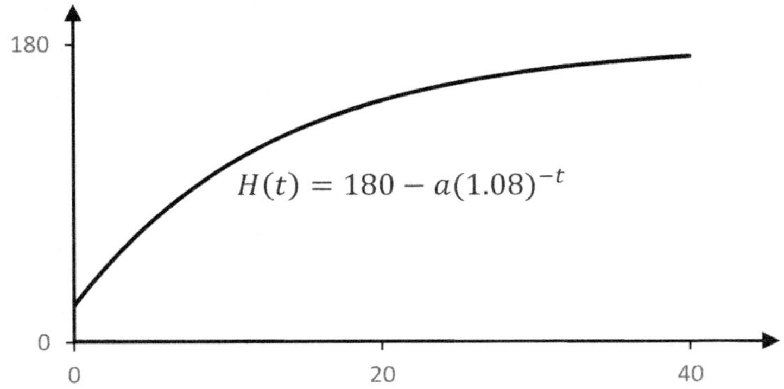

(a) Write down what the value of 180 represents in the context of the question.[2]

The temperature in the oven/the maximum possible temperature of the cake mix.

(b) The temperature in the centre of the cake mix was 22°C when placed in the oven. Find the value of a. [2]

$22 = 180 - a(1.08)^{-0} \Rightarrow a = 180 - 22 = 158$

(c) The cake is removed from the oven 29 minutes after the temperature in the centre of the cake has reached 150°C.

Find the total time that the baking tin is the oven. Give your answers to 3 significant figures. [3]

$$150 = 180 - 158 \times (1.08)^{-t} \Rightarrow t = -\frac{\ln \frac{180 - 150}{158}}{\ln 1.08} = 21.6 \text{ min}$$

The total time that the baking tin is the oven is:

$21.6 + 29 = 50.6$ min

Section B: Mechanics

9 A wooden crate rests on a rough horizontal surface. The coefficient of friction between the crate and the surface is 0.8. A boy attempts to move a wooden crate. When he applied a horizontal force of 150 N, the crate is on the point of moving.

(a) Find the mass of the crate. Give your answer to 3 decimal places. [2]

$$150 = 0.8\,mg \Rightarrow m = \frac{150}{0.8 \times 9.8} = 19.133 \text{ kg}$$

(b) Instead, the boy use a handle to pull the crate forward. He exerts a force of 150 N, at an angle of $30°$ above the horizontal, as shown in the diagram. What acceleration must the boy have in order to do this? Give your answer to 3 decimal places. [3]

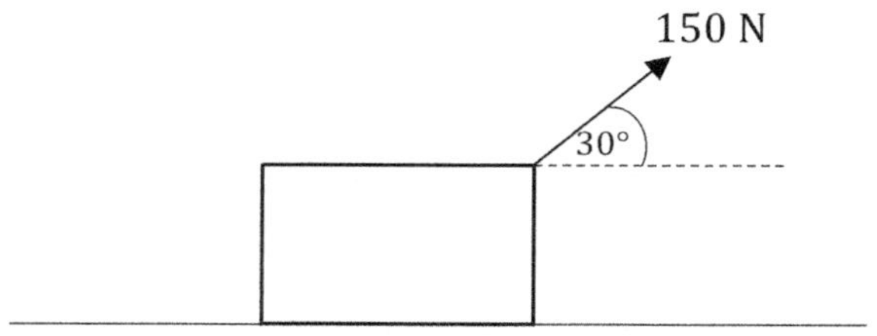

$$P - F = ma \Rightarrow 150\cos 30° - \mu(mg - 150\sin 30°) = ma \Rightarrow$$

$$a = \frac{150\cos 30° - \mu(mg - 150\sin 30°)}{m}$$

$$= \frac{150 \times \frac{\sqrt{3}}{2} - 0.8mg + 0.8 \times 150 \times \frac{1}{2}}{19.133}$$

$$= \frac{75\sqrt{3} - 150 + 60}{19.133} = 2.086 \text{ m s}^{-2}$$

10 The height, h metres, of an object that is moving along a vertical path is given by the function $h = 112 + 96t - 16t^2$, where t is the time, in seconds.

(a) Find the maximum height of the object and the time at which it reaches maximum height. [3]

$$h = 112 + 96t - 16t^2 = 112 - 16(t^2 - 6t) = 112 - 16(t-3)^2 + 16 \times 9$$

$$= 256 - 16(t-3)^2 \le 256$$

The maximum height of the object is 256 m at $t = 3$ s.

Alternative method:

$\frac{\mathrm{d}h}{\mathrm{d}t} = 0 \Rightarrow 96 - 32t = 0 \Rightarrow t = 3\ \mathrm{s}$

$\frac{\mathrm{d}^2h}{\mathrm{d}t^2} = -32 < 0$

The maximum height of the object is at $t = 3$ s

$h = 112 + 96 \times 3 - 16 \times 3^2 = 256$ m

(b) Find the object's velocity when its height is 0 metre. [3]

$112 + 96t - 16t^2 = 0 \Rightarrow 7 + 6t - t^2 = 0 \Rightarrow t^2 - 6t - 7 = 0 \Rightarrow$

$(t + 1)(t - 7) = 0$

$t = 7$ is its solution, as $t \geq 0$

Its height is 0 metre at $t = 7$ s

$\frac{\mathrm{d}h}{\mathrm{d}t} = 96 - 32t = 96 - 32 \times 7 = -128$

The object's velocity is $-128\ \mathrm{m\ s^{-1}}$, when its height is 0 metre.

11 A woman of mass 60 kg is standing in a lift and the lift has a mass of 340 kg. Find the tension in the cable supporting the lift and the force exerted on the woman by the lift by when

(a) the lift is at rest [4]

As the lift is at rest the forces must be in equilibrium. T is the tension in the cable, m is the total mass of the woman, the lift and m_w is the mass of the woman and F is the force exerted on the woman by the lift. Therefore we have

$m = 60 + 340 = 400$ kg

$T - mg = 0 \Rightarrow T = mg = 400 \times 9.8 = 3920$ N

$F - m_w g = m_w a \Rightarrow F = m_w g + m_w a = 60 \times 9.8 + 60 \times 0 = 588$ N

(b) the lift is moving at constant speed [2]

The forces on the lift must be in equilibrium, because it is moving at a constant speed, so the tension is 3920 N, and is the same as that when the lift is at rest.

$T = 3920$ N

In the same way, the force exerted on the woman by the lift is the same as that when the lift is at rest.

$F = 588$ N

(c) the lift is accelerating upwards at 0.9 m s^{-2} [4]

$T - mg = ma \Rightarrow T = mg + ma = 400 \times 9.8 + 400 \times 0.9 = 4280$ N

$F - m_w g = m_w a \Rightarrow F = m_w g + m_w a = 60 \times 9.8 + 60 \times 0.9 = 642$ N

(d) the lift is accelerating downwards at 0.5 m s^{-2}. [4]

Here $a = -0.5$ m s^{-2} because the acceleration is downwards.

$T - mg = ma \Rightarrow T = mg + ma = 400 \times 9.8 - 400 \times 0.5 = 3720$ N

$F - m_w g = m_w a \Rightarrow F = m_w g + m_w a = 60 \times 9.8 - 60 \times 0.5 = 558$ N

Printed in Great Britain
by Amazon

25449360R00046